# THE NEW PASTA COOKBOOK

## JOANNE GLYNN

TORMONT

# CONTENTS

~

BEGINNINGS ~ 10

FAST PASTA ~ 30

SAUCES ~ 44

FINE FARE ~ 54

ENDINGS ~ 88

MEASURING MADE EASY ~ 95

INDEX ~ 96

*This edition is published with the permission of HarperCollins Publishers Pty Limited.*

*Published in 1993 by*
*Tormont Publications Inc.*
*338 Saint Antoine St. East*
*Montreal, Canada H2Y 1A3*
*Tel. (514) 954-1441*
*Fax (514) 954-1443*
*ISBN 2-89429-393-3*
*Printed in Canada*

*Photography: Ashley Barber*
*Food Styling: Michelle Gorry*

*Front cover photograph by Rowan Fotheringham with styling by Donna Hay (Spicy Ricotta Agnolotti in Herb Leaf Pasta, recipe on page 58).*

# THE PASTA STORY

Pasta's popularity has always been its adaptability. It can come in many different forms, with taste differences and visual variety; it is cheap, quickly and easily prepared; it can be a meal in itself or eaten with other foods such as meat and vegetables. Pasta has a high nutritional value and is an easily digested source of energy.

Pasta is a dough made from flour, water and/or eggs. The flour used for commercial pasta is made from milled durum wheat in the form of semolina, a coarsely ground meal. Dough made from durum wheat semolina absorbs less water and will dry easily; holds together well during kneading, drying and cooking; withstands pressure well; has a better texture and 'bite' and reheats successfully.

Eggs are sometimes added to commercial dried pasta to give extra body and flavor. Homemade pasta nearly always uses eggs, which give the dough flavor and make it manageable and easy to roll.

### BUYING PASTA

Prepared pasta falls into three main categories:

PACKAGED DRY PASTA (*pasta secche*) which is available from every supermarket. It is worth checking the labels to establish that durum wheat semolina has been used (*pasta di semolina di grano duro* on Italian imports) and for the use or exclusion of egg (*all' uovo* means with eggs). Cooking time for this pasta is 10 minutes or more as it needs to rehydrate as well as cook.

FRESH PASTA (*pasta fresca*) is available from specialty pasta shops and delicatessens and in the refrigerator in some supermarkets. It is usually displayed in bulk so you can purchase as little or as much as you need. This pasta is quite pliable and takes a very short time to cook (1½ to 3 minutes).

DRIED, PREPACKED "FRESH PASTA" falls between the other two categories and is available from supermarkets and specialty stores. Cooking time is 3 to 5 minutes.

### HINTS ON COOKING

The success of a pasta dish depends on the correct cooking of the pasta you have chosen to use.

First, the proportion of water to pasta is important. Too little, and the pasta will be crowded and unable to cook evenly. It will become gluey as the relatively small amount of water becomes starch-laden. There can never be too much water. Use a minimum of 1 gallon (4 L) water to every 1 lb (450 g) pasta; use more if cooking dried pasta, as it absorbs more water.

Use a very large pot. Bring the water to a rolling boil. Just before putting in the pasta add a dash of oil (to help prevent sticking) and a large pinch of salt (or a knob of rock salt or unrefined sea salt) to help bring out the flavor. If using fresh pasta, shake it gently to loosen the strands before adding it to the water.

Once the pasta is in, stir to move it off the bottom of the pot. When the water comes back to a boil start timing, maintaining a slow rolling boil. Don't stir too often, as this tends to release excess starch.

The pasta is done when it is *al dente* – tender, but with some resistance to the bite. You should feel the texture and form in the mouth, not mushy dough.

If the pasta is overcooked it cannot physically support the rest of the ingredients and won't allow for an even distribution of the sauce. Taste the pasta just before the time is up. Note: As fresh pasta takes only a couple of minutes to cook, its timing is more critical.

Don't be overzealous about draining, as it is desirable to leave a little of the cooking water to help with lubrication. Only rinse if the pasta is to be in used in a cold dish.

Next, stir in a little oil or melted butter. This helps with the final saucing and keeps the pasta from sticking together. Finally, always have the waiting bowls or serving dishes warmed.

## HOMEMADE PASTA

All-purpose flour is usually used when making egg pasta. It gives a fine-textured, light dough that is well suited to filled pastas such as ravioli, as it gives the pasta good elasticity.

The addition of durum wheat semolina gives a better color, more flavor and a resilient texture, as well as providing the nutritional benefits of hard wheat flours. The proportion of semolina to all-purpose flour is a matter of choice, but a maximum of two-thirds semolina and one-third all-purpose flour is recommended. If you are making pasta with other flours such as whole-wheat or buckwheat, remember that different grinds and grains have different absorption levels and qualities of elasticity.

Eggs used should be the freshest available, as their freshness influences not only the flavor and color of the pasta, but also the elastic quality of the dough.

The standard proportion of eggs to flour is 1 medium egg to every ¼ cup (185 mL) flour, and a pinch of salt is generally added. It is sometimes necessary to use a little water, but this will depend on the particular flours used and the humidity at the time. Eggless pasta is made the same way as egg pasta except that the eggs are replaced in volume by water.

The only equipment you need is a board and a long rolling pin. However, a food processor takes the labor out of mixing, and a hand-cranked pasta machine simplifies and takes the guesswork out of rolling and cutting.

For a basic dough, you need 1½ cups (375 mL) all-purpose flour, 2 eggs, a large pinch of salt and some water. This amount is enough to make two main courses or three entrées.

**MIXING BY HAND** Use a pastry board or a large bowl. Put flour in a mound with a well in the center. Add eggs and salt, and start blending with a fork or fingers, incorporating more and more of the flour into the eggs and working from the inside outward. When flour and eggs are combined, start to knead the dough on the board, incorporating extra flour or adding water as necessary.

It will take about 5 minutes to get a smooth, firm dough. If durum wheat semolina is used, allow a good 7 to 10 minutes of kneading. It takes this long for the hard semolina to absorb moisture and develop its strong, pliable characteristics.

Only experience can tell you when the dough is ready. It should not be sticky or wet to the touch. If you can knead it well without adding flour, it is probably ready.

When finished, cover the dough with a tea towel or upturned bowl to prevent a crust forming, and let it stand for at least 15 minutes.

**MIXING IN A PROCESSOR** Use the metal blade. Add dry ingredients to the bowl. With the motor running, add eggs through the feed tube. After 5 seconds a ball should form. If the dough is still sticky, add flour until a ball forms or the machine slows down or stops. In some cases a few drops of water may be necessary to take the dough from the mealy stage. Take the dough out and knead it until elastic, 2 to 3 minutes. Rest dough as above.

### ROLLING AND CUTTING BY HAND

Divide the dough into manageable balls and keep them covered until needed. Working ball by ball, press out the center with your hand. Using a long rolling pin, roll each evenly and smoothly on a board lightly dusted with flour.

Lift and turn the dough often, and don't be in a hurry; you want an even, thinly rolled sheet of pasta. The pasta will swell a little with cooking, so roll it thinner than the desired cooked thickness. For filled pastas the dough should be almost paper thin.

When you're happy with the proportions, cover each sheet with a layer of plastic wrap, then cover with a damp tea towel to prevent drying out.

If the dough is to be cut into strips like tagliatelle, let it dry slightly; this prevents the ribbons from sticking together. Then cut the sheets into rectangles approximately 10 inches (25 cm) long and roll these up, jelly roll style, along their length. Using a sharp knife and with smooth strokes, cut uniform slices that unroll to become, for example, tagliatelle, ¼ inch (0.5 cm) wide, pappardelle, ¾ inch (2 cm) wide, or whatever pasta type you decide to make.

**ROLLING AND CUTTING WITH PASTA MACHINE** Starting with the rollers on the widest setting, roll a flattened ball of dough through two or three times. Fold the dough in thirds and roll again. Repeat this process four or five times or until the dough is a smooth and elastic sheet of even proportions. Now pass the dough through the rollers with them set at decreasing widths apart, until the desired thickness is reached. Try to avoid adding flour, but if dough becomes sticky, a light dusting should help it through.

If, before cutting, the dough seems too wet, let it sit, uncovered, for 15 minutes or so. It should be dry enough so that the cut lengths won't stick together but will still pass through the cutters without cracking. Crank the sheets of dough through the required cutting rollers.

Spread the cut lengths on a dry tea towel, or hang them over the backs of chairs or a broom handle until ready to cook. Pasta made entirely with all-purpose flour

*Try a combination of semolina and flour*

*Making your own pasta is easy and fun*

doesn't dry well; it tends to crack as the moisture evaporates.

**MAKING FILLED PASTA** The thinly rolled sheets should be kept under a damp tea towel or pieces of plastic wrap and used quickly.

Have the filling ready before the pasta so you're ready to go as soon as the dough is made.

There are three main ways of making filled shapes:

i) Using a Mold: these are trays pressed with the grooves and ridges of different shaped and sized ravioli, which usually come with their own little rolling pin to seal and cut the dough around the filling. They are useful when a uniformly sized and cut pasta is desired.

ii) Sheeted Filling: this is a successful way of making many ravioli quickly. Cut two sheets of dough, one slightly bigger than the other. On the smaller sheet place spoonfuls of filling at even intervals, then brush along the intended cutting lines with beaten egg. Position the larger sheet of pasta over the top neatly and run over the cutting lines with your finger to make sure that both sheets of pasta are touching together. Now cut the shapes out with a floured pastry wheel. The best one to use is a cutter-crimper that cuts and seals at the same time. A zigzag wheel is also effective.

iii) Folded by Hand: this method gives a well-sealed ravioli as each one is pressed together by hand.

Working with one sheet of pasta at a time, cut out the shapes required (round for a half-moon ravioli; squares for triangles; rectangles for squares) and brush the borders with beaten egg.

*Roll out pasta smoothly and evenly with a rolling pin*

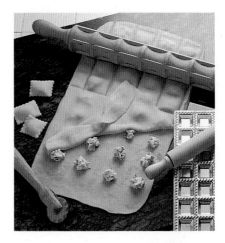

*Special pasta making equipment makes the task easy*

Place a spoonful of filling to one side of the center line of each. Fold the dough over the filling to match corresponding edges, press between the fingers and then seal the cut edge with a pastry cutter.

Place finished stuffed pasta on a tray or plate dusted with semolina or rice flour and store in the refrigerator before cooking.

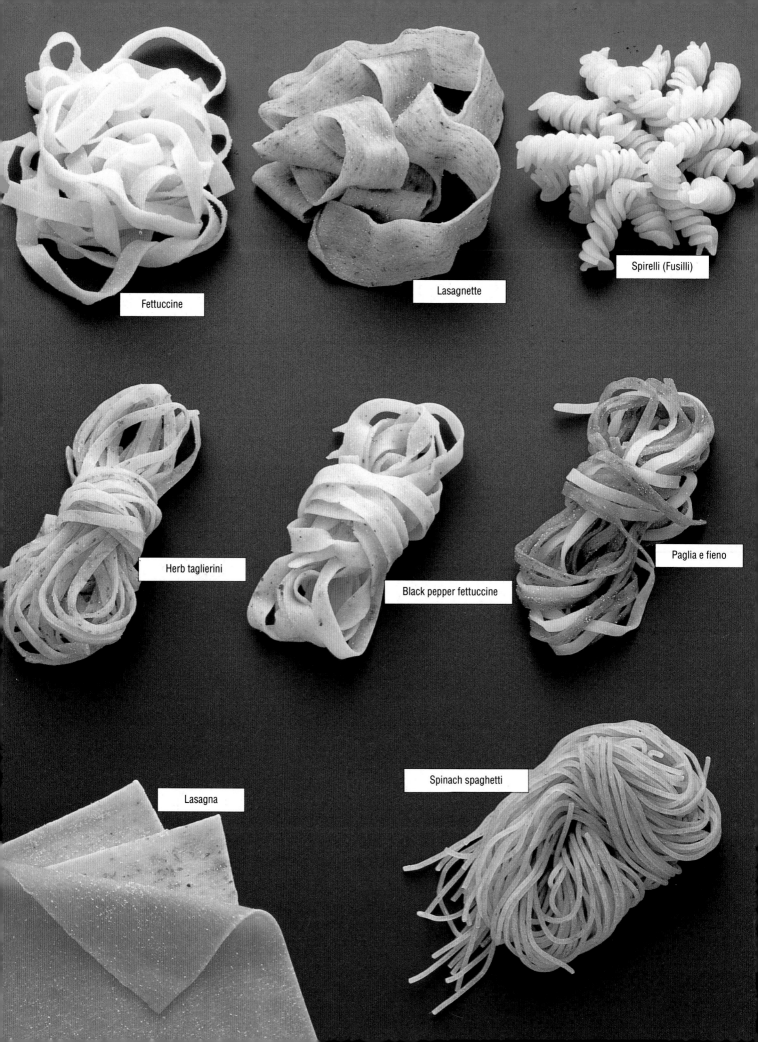

Fettuccine

Lasagnette

Spirelli (Fusilli)

Herb taglierini

Black pepper fettuccine

Paglia e fieno

Lasagna

Spinach spaghetti

Fresh Pasta – for taste, texture, temptation.

Today an integral part of a truly balanced diet.

Cooks in minutes for that minimum-effort, maximum-result meal.

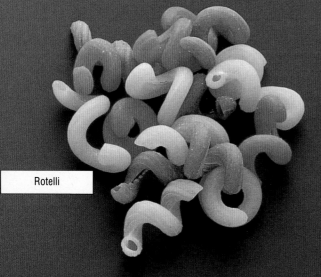

Rotelli

Conchiglie

Fettuccine – tomato, spinach and egg

Egg spaghetti

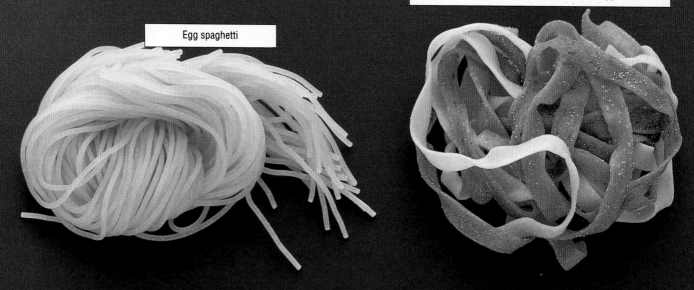

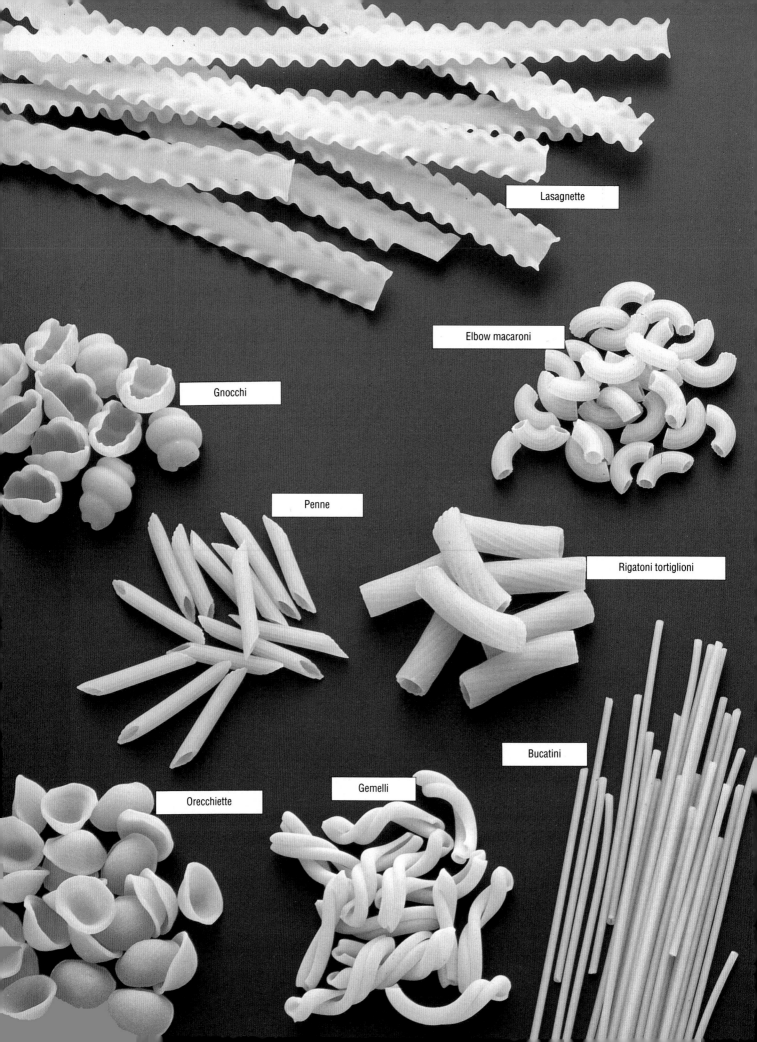

Lasagnette

Elbow macaroni

Gnocchi

Penne

Rigatoni tortiglioni

Bucatini

Orecchiette

Gemelli

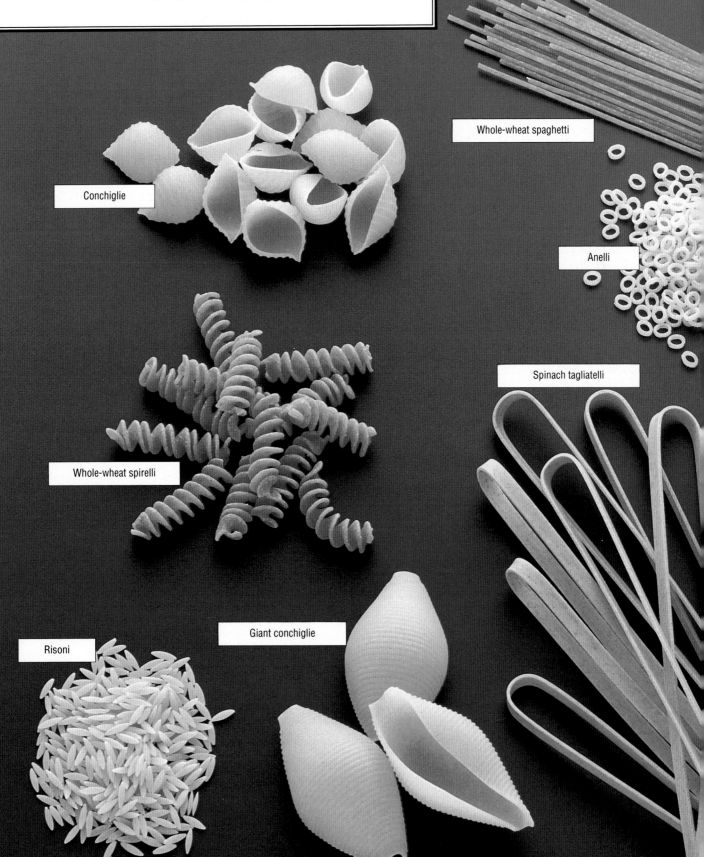

Dried pasta is available in more shapes and sizes than there are days of the year – rings for soups, rolled sheets for baked dishes, large shells for stuffing and all those long lengths for tempting sauces.

Conchiglie

Whole-wheat spaghetti

Anelli

Spinach tagliatelli

Whole-wheat spirelli

Giant conchiglie

Risoni

What better way to start a meal than with a bowl of pasta, delicately sauced or tossed with other flavorful ingredients? Pasta takes so many forms and guises that there is always something appropriate to serve. Many of these recipes make excellent light meals served with a salad.

≈ **SERVING PASTA**

*Some dishes rely on a small, subtle coating of the pasta, while others require the pasta to be secondary to a hearty sauce. As a guideline, allow ¼ lb (110 g) of dried pasta per adult for a main meal and 2 – 2½ oz (60 – 70 g) for an entrée or small helping. If cooking fresh or homemade pasta, ⅓ lb (150 g) is a good main course serving; 3 – 3½ oz (80 – 100 g) for an entrée. And what you don't finish can always be eaten the following day!*

## SHRIMP AND BASIL SOUP

3 tbsp (45 mL) olive oil

1½ tbsp (20 mL) butter

2 cloves garlic

1 small red onion, thinly sliced

2 stalks celery, cut in ¾ – 1¼ inch (2 – 3 cm) strips

3 small carrots, thinly sliced

1 tbsp (15 mL) finely chopped fresh parsley

2 tbsp (30 mL) finely chopped fresh basil

salt and freshly ground black pepper

pinch cayenne pepper

1 lb (450 g) medium uncooked shrimp, peeled and deveined

½ cup (125 mL) medium dry sherry

4 cups (1 L) chicken stock

2½ oz (70 g) small conchiglie

¼ cup (60 mL) cream

fresh basil to garnish

**1** In a large saucepan heat oil and butter. Add garlic cloves and onion and sauté gently for 2 to 3 minutes.

**2** Add celery and carrots and fry until vegetables are golden; do not brown. Toss in parsley and basil and season to taste. Stir briefly, add shrimp, toss, then remove garlic cloves.

**3** Pour in sherry, increase heat and cook for 2 to 3 minutes. Add chicken stock, bring to the boil then simmer for 5 minutes.

**4** Add conchiglie and simmer until pasta is *al dente*.

**5** Stir in cream, adjust seasonings to taste and serve garnished with basil leaves.

**SERVES 4**

## BROCCOLI SOUP

3 tbsp (45 mL) olive oil

1 large onion, thinly sliced

2 oz (55 g) diced prosciutto or unsmoked ham

1 clove garlic, crushed

5 cups (1.25 L) chicken stock

2 oz (55 g) stellini or other pastina (tiny pasta shapes)

½ lb (225 g) broccoli, tops cut into small florets and the tender stems julienned

salt and freshly ground black pepper

freshly grated Parmesan cheese

**1** Heat oil in a large pan and gently sauté onion, prosciutto and garlic for 4 to 5 minutes.

**2** Pour in stock, bring to the boil and simmer, partly covered, for 10 minutes.

**3** Add stellini and broccoli and cook until pasta is *al dente* and broccoli crisp but tender. Season to taste. Serve in warm bowls and sprinkle with Parmesan.

**SERVES 4**

# PUMPKIN AND LEEK SOUP

1½ lbs (680 g) pumpkin pieces, skin left on

¼ cup (60 mL) butter

2 leeks, white part only, thinly sliced

1 large Spanish onion, chopped

¾ lb (340 g) potatoes, peeled and diced

2 cups (500 mL) milk

2 cups (500 mL) chicken stock

2½ oz (70 g) risoni or orzo

salt and white pepper

pinch cayenne pepper

1 cup (250 mL) cream

1 tbsp (15 mL) finely chopped fresh mint

**1**  Preheat oven to 375°F (190°C).

**2**  Place pumpkin pieces skin side up and close together in a large baking dish. Pour ½ cup (125 mL) water over pumpkin and bake for about 1 hour.

**3**  Melt half the butter and gently fry leeks until softened. Remove from the pan and fry onion and potatoes in remaining butter until golden. Add milk and boil gently for 20 minutes. Don't worry if the milk reduces; just make sure there is enough liquid to keep vegetables from sticking to the pan.

**4**  When pumpkin is tender and golden, remove from oven, cool, then remove skin and any excessively browned surfaces.

**5**  In the meantime put chicken stock on to boil, add risoni and cook until barely done. Remove pasta with a slotted spoon and set aside with leeks. Reserve stock.

**6**  Now blend pumpkin and potato mixture in a food processor or force through a fine sieve. Season with salt, pepper and cayenne to taste.

**7**  Transfer to a clean saucepan and blend in the hot stock. Add cream, bring to a boil, then stir in leeks and pasta. If the soup is too thick, thin it with extra stock or water. Adjust seasoning and stir in mint.

**SERVES 4 TO 6**

*Pumpkin and Leek Soup*

# SPINACH FUSILLI AND ZUCCHINI SALAD

*If fresh bocconcini aren't available, don't substitute ordinary mozzarella; choose a fresh, white cheese such as feta or stracchino.*

⅓ lb (150 g) spinach fusilli

¼ lb (110 g) small zucchini, sliced

4 anchovy fillets, soaked in milk for 45 minutes

2½ cups (625 mL) celery, sliced, plus some coarsely torn tender leaves

1 cup (250 mL) cherry tomatoes or small tomatoes cut into wedges

⅓ lb (150 g) bocconcini, cut into small pieces

1 tbsp (15 mL) fresh basil leaves, roughly torn

### DRESSING

⅓ cup (85 mL) white wine vinegar

¼ cup (60 mL) olive oil

salt and freshly ground black pepper

**1**  Cook fusilli in boiling salted water until just *al dente*. Drain, rinse under cold water and drain again. Transfer to a salad bowl and stir a little vegetable oil into the pasta.

**2**  Sprinkle zucchini with a little salt and let stand in a strainer for 30 minutes. Rinse, drain and add to the pasta.

**3**  Pat dry the anchovy fillets, reserve two for decoration and cut the others into small pieces. Add to the salad bowl with celery and leaves, tomatoes, bocconcini and basil.

**4  TO PREPARE DRESSING:** Combine vinegar, oil, salt and pepper in a jar, shaking well. Dress the salad, tossing lightly to coat. Garnish with reserved anchovies, cover with plastic wrap and refrigerate for at least 1½ hours before serving.

**SERVES 4**

≈ **PUMPKIN AND LEEK SOUP**

*Baking the pumpkin gives it a special mellow flavor, but if you're pushed for time it can be peeled and boiled with the potatoes.*

≈ **BOCCONCINI**

*These are little balls of mozzarella with a life of 4 to 5 days. They are eaten for their own sake and usually not used as a melting cheese. Don't substitute matured mozzarella for bocconcini.*

# SALAD TRICOLORE

½ lb (225 g) fresh tomato rotelli or
6½ oz (180 g) dried

1 tsp (5 mL) peanut oil

½ lb (225 g) sliced cooked chicken

¼ cup (60 mL) sesame seeds, toasted

1 large bunch spinach or Swiss chard,
rinsed and dried, torn into pieces

1 bunch green onions, sliced thinly,
including green parts

### DRESSING

¼ cup (60 mL) peanut oil

¼ cup (60 mL) olive oil

¼ cup (60 mL) soy sauce

¼ cup (60 mL) rice wine vinegar

1½ – 2½ tbsp (20 – 40 mL) sugar

salt and freshly ground black pepper

**1** Cook pasta in boiling salted water until *al dente*. Drain, rinse under cold water and drain again. Put in a large salad bowl and stir in peanut oil. Cool.

**2** Add chicken and sesame seeds.

**3** TO PREPARE DRESSING: In a jar combine all dressing ingredients and shake well.

**4** Pour dressing over salad. Cover and chill for at least 2 hours.

**5** To serve, toss green onions and spinach through the salad.

**SERVES 4 TO 6**

# RICOTTA GNOCCHETTI

¾ lb (340 g) dry ricotta cheese

1¼ cups (310 mL) all-purpose flour

3 tbsp (45 mL) fine white bread crumbs

1½ cups (375 mL) grated Parmesan cheese

2 eggs plus 2 egg yolks, beaten together

salt, white pepper and nutmeg

⅓ cup (85 mL) butter

**1** In a bowl combine ricotta, flour, bread crumbs, half the Parmesan and eggs. Add a pinch each of the seasonings and blend to form a smooth dough that is dry to the touch. It may be necessary to add a little more flour or a few drops of milk to get the right balance, depending on the moistness of the ricotta.

**2** Knead the dough well, then let it rest, loosely covered, for 15 minutes. Using your hands, roll the dough into two or three long ropes, ½ inch (1 cm) in diameter. Again let it rest for 15 minutes before slicing diagonally into ¾ inch (2 cm) lengths.

**3** Cook gnocchi in boiling unsalted water for 3 minutes. In the meantime melt butter and cook over low heat until golden brown. Drain gnocchi and pile on a warm serving plate. Pour butter over gnocchi and sprinkle with remaining Parmesan before serving.

**SERVES 4**

# TUNA GNOCCHI SALAD

½ lb (225 g) broccoli, broken into florets

½ lb (225 g) cauliflower, broken into florets

½ lb (225 g) dried gnocchi shells
(pasta shapes, not dumplings)

1 bunch green onions, sliced, including
some of the green parts

4 small tomatoes, cut into wedges

1 clove garlic, thinly sliced

¼ cup (60 mL) finely chopped fresh
Italian parsley

½ cup (125 mL) extra virgin olive oil

juice of 1 small lemon

½ tsp (2.5 mL) sea salt

freshly ground black pepper

1 lb (450 g) canned tuna, packed
in oil, drained

**1** Bring a large saucepan of water to the boil, add a pinch of salt and add the broccoli and cauliflower. Cook for 2 to 3 minutes; vegetables should be still crisp and not soft. Remove from the pan with a slotted spoon and rinse under cold water. Shake them dry and transfer to a large serving bowl.

**2** To the same boiling water add pasta and cook for 15 minutes, or until *al dente*. Rinse under cold water and shake dry. Transfer to the salad bowl.

**3** Add green onions, tomatoes, garlic, parsley, olive oil, lemon juice, salt and pepper to the bowl and mix together lightly.

**4** Coarsely flake tuna into bite-size pieces, add to salad and toss. Serve at room temperature.

**SERVES 4 AS A LIGHT MEAL**

# BEAN AND PASTA SALAD

½ lb (225 g) pennette or other
small hollow pasta

3 cups (750 mL) cooked cannellini beans
(or any small white beans)

1 small red onion, thinly sliced

1 thin stalk celery, sliced

2 small tomatoes, cut in wedges

2 oz (60 g) small black olives

fresh oregano leaves, to garnish

### DRESSING

½ cup (125 mL) extra virgin olive oil

1½ tsp (7.5 mL) Dijon-style mustard

juice of 1 lemon

1 tbsp (15 mL) finely chopped fresh oregano
or parsley

salt and freshly ground black pepper

1 clove garlic, crushed

**1** Cook pennette in boiling salted water until *al dente*. Drain, rinse under cold water and drain again. Transfer to a large serving bowl, stir in a little of the oil to prevent sticking, and cool.

**2** Add beans, onion, celery, tomatoes and olives.

**3 TO PREPARE DRESSING:** Combine all dressing ingredients in a jar and shake well.

**4** Pour dressing over salad. Toss thoroughly and taste for salt and pepper. Cover and chill. When ready to serve, toss again lightly and garnish with oregano leaves.

**SERVES 4**

# SAFFRON RISONI SALAD

¾ lb (340 g) risoni

½ cup (125 mL) olive oil

½ tsp (2.5 mL) pure saffron powder

1 cup (250 mL) pine nuts

½ cup (125 mL) currants

2 cloves garlic, crushed

juice of 1 lemon

¼ tsp (1 mL) ground cumin

1 tsp (5 mL) ground turmeric

½ tsp (2.5 mL) sugar

salt and freshly ground black pepper

1 small green pepper, sliced into ½ – ¾ inch
(1 – 2 cm) lengths

3 tbsp (45 mL) finely chopped fresh parsley

3 tbsp (45 mL) finely chopped fresh mint

3 tbsp (45 mL) finely chopped fresh
coriander

coriander leaves, for garnish

**1** Cook risoni in boiling salted water for a minute or two less than recommended. Drain, rinse in cold water and drain again. Stir in a little olive oil to prevent sticking.

**2** Heat oil in a small pan and add saffron, pine nuts and currants. Cook gently until nuts are toasted and saffron gives off its unique aroma. Remove from heat and add garlic, lemon juice, cumin, turmeric, sugar, salt and pepper to taste. Let stand for at least 5 minutes.

**3** Add green pepper, herbs and pine nut mixture to the pasta. Toss before serving and garnish with coriander leaves.

**SERVES 4 TO 6 AS A SIDE DISH**

≈ **SAFFRON
RISONI SALAD**

*This delicious spicy "rice" salad is slightly sweet and is a perfect accompaniment for broiled or barbecued meats.*

# PASTRAMI, MUSHROOM AND CUCUMBER SALAD

*Pastrami is made from a lean cut of beef, so this dish is low in calories and high in protein and vitamins.*

½ lb (225 g) lasagnette, broken into quarters

½ lb (225 g) pastrami, cut in strips

1 stalk celery, sliced

2 small tomatoes, cut in wedges

1 English cucumber, about 12 inches (30 cm) long, thinly sliced

¾ cup (185 mL) mushrooms, thinly sliced

¼ tsp (1 mL) finely chopped fresh coriander, for garnish

### DRESSING

¼ cup (60 mL) olive oil

3 tbsp (45 mL) red wine vinegar

½ tsp (2.5 mL) Dijon-style mustard

salt and freshly ground black pepper

1 clove garlic, crushed

¼ tsp (1 mL) hot chili oil

**1** Cook lasagnette in boiling salted water until *al dente*; drain and rinse under cold water, then drain again before transferring to a salad bowl.

**2** To the salad bowl add pastrami, celery, tomato wedges, cucumber and mushrooms.

**3 TO PREPARE DRESSING:** Combine dressing ingredients in a jar and shake well to blend.

**4** Toss the dressing through the salad and refrigerate, covered, for several hours.

**5** Adjust seasoning and sprinkle with fresh coriander before serving.

**SERVES 4**

# TUNA, GREEN BEAN AND ONION SALAD

*This salad is equally good served warm or refrigerated overnight and served the next day.*

½ lb (225 g) green beans, trimmed and cut in 1¼ inch (3 cm) lengths

⅔ lb (300 g) short pasta shapes (fusilli or penne rigate)

½ cup (125 mL) olive oil

½ lb (225 g) fresh tuna fillet, sliced in 1¼ – 1½ inch (3 – 4 cm) pieces

1 red onion, thinly sliced

1 tsp (5 mL) balsamic vinegar

salt and freshly ground black pepper

**1** In a large pan of boiling water, cook beans for 1 to 2 minutes until tender-crisp. Remove with a slotted spoon and rinse under cold water. Drain and transfer to a serving bowl.

**2** Add a pinch of salt to the boiling water and cook pasta until *al dente*. Drain, rinse under cold water then drain again before adding to beans.

**3** In a frying pan heat half the oil. Add tuna and onion. Sauté until tuna is just cooked through. Add vinegar, turn up heat and quickly cook until dressing is reduced and lightly coats tuna. Transfer tuna and onion to the salad bowl, leaving behind any bits on the bottom of the pan.

**4** Toss beans, pasta, tuna and onion together lightly and mix with remaining oil. Add salt and pepper to taste. Cool to room temperature before serving.

**SERVES 4**

*Tuna, Green Bean and Onion Salad (above) and Pastrami, Mushroom and Cucumber Salad (below)*

≈ **PASTINA**

*Pastina is the generic term for all tiny pasta shapes usually served in soups.*

# STUFFED PEPPERS AND TOMATOES

*The peppers and tomatoes can be eaten hot or cold and can be served as a first course, a light meal or part of a buffet. They are a good accompaniment to lamb, veal or chicken.*

**3 large tomatoes, stem ends sliced off**

**3 green peppers, stem ends and seeds removed**

**4–5 tbsp (60–75 mL) chicken or vegetable stock**

### FILLING

**3 tbsp (45 mL) olive oil**

**1 large onion, chopped**

**2 cloves garlic, crushed**

**¼ tsp (1 mL) cayenne pepper**

**salt and freshly ground black pepper**

**1 tbsp (15 mL) currants**

**1 tbsp (15 mL) pine nuts**

**1 tbsp (15 mL) chopped fresh coriander**

**1 tsp (5 mL) chopped fresh parsley**

**1½ cups (375 mL) cooked risoni or other tiny pasta shapes**

**1 cup (250 mL) grated aged Cheddar or Emmenthaler cheese**

**1** Preheat oven to 350°F (180°C).

**2 TO PREPARE FILLING:** Heat oil and gently sauté onion and garlic until soft. Add cayenne, salt and pepper to taste, currants, pine nuts, coriander and parsley. Sauté until nuts are light brown. Transfer to a bowl and combine with pasta and cheese.

**3** Scoop pulp from tomatoes, chop finely and add to filling. Mix well.

**4** Divide filling between peppers and tomatoes, stuffing lightly. Put peppers into a shallow ovenproof dish, pour 1 tbsp (15 mL) stock over each and bake for 30 minutes.

**5** Add tomatoes to the dish and bake for 20 minutes more, or until tender.

**SERVES 6**

# LUMACHE WITH ARTICHOKES

**¼ cup (60 mL) olive oil**

**1 large onion, roughly chopped**

**2 cloves garlic, crushed**

**1 tbsp (15 mL) dried basil**

**2 tbsp (30 mL) chopped fresh parsley**

**pinch chili powder**

**1 tsp (5 mL) dried oregano**

**6½ cups (1.6 L) canned Italian peeled tomatoes, drained, juice reserved**

**¼ tsp (1 mL) salt**

**¾ lb (340 g) lumache, pipe rigate or other multi-surfaced shape**

**1¾ cups (440 mL) canned artichoke hearts, drained, juice reserved**

**3 tbsp (45 mL) grated pecorino cheese**

**1** Heat oil in a large pot and sauté onion, garlic, basil, parsley, chili and oregano for 5 minutes.

**2** Roughly chop tomatoes and add them to the pot with the salt. Simmer, uncovered, for about 45 minutes, or until reduced and very thick. Add reserved tomato and artichoke juices, stir well and simmer 15 minutes more.

**3** Cook lumache in boiling salted water until *al dente*.

**4** Cut each artichoke heart into six and stir the pieces into the sauce. Add pecorino and stir.

**5** Drain cooked pasta and add to sauce. Stir well, transfer to warm dishes and serve with extra cheese.

**SERVES 4**

**PORCINI MUSHROOMS**

*The unforgettable taste of fresh porcini or boletus mushrooms cooked in butter is closely matched by using a combination of the dried variety and fresh plump button mushrooms. Choose large ones with lots of white flesh to duplicate the texture and appearance of fresh porcini.*

# LINGUINE WITH MUSHROOMS

½ oz (14 g) dried porcini or
boletus mushrooms

2 tbsp (30 mL) butter

1 small onion, finely chopped

1 lb (450 g) very large button
mushrooms, sliced

1 tbsp (15 mL) chopped fresh sage
(don't substitute dried)

1 tbsp (15 mL) finely chopped fresh parsley

salt and freshly ground black pepper

1 lb (450 g) fresh linguine or
⅔ lb (300 g) dried

⅓ cup (85 mL) freshly grated
Parmesan cheese

**1**  Soak porcini mushrooms in ¾ cup
(185 mL) warm water for 45 to 60 minutes.
Drain off liquid and filter it through muslin
or a paper coffee filter to remove grit. Finely
slice the rehydrated mushrooms.

**2**  Melt half the butter in a frying pan and
gently sauté onion until soft and golden.
Add porcini and filtered mushroom liquid
and cook until liquid has evaporated. Add
remaining butter, button mushrooms and
herbs. Season well and gently simmer,
covered, for 15 to 20 minutes.

**3**  Meanwhile, cook pasta in boiling salted
water until *al dente*; drain and toss with the
sauce and Parmesan.

**SERVES 4**

# SPINACH PASTA FRITTATA

½ cup (125 mL) grated Parmesan cheese

5 eggs

½ cup (125 mL) milk

½ cup (125 mL) cream

1 tbsp (15 mL) olive oil

1 tbsp (15 mL) all-purpose flour

salt and pepper

½ lb (225 g) cooked spinach spaghetti or
fettuccine

2 tsp (10 mL) chopped fresh herbs
(parsley, oregano, chives)

1 tbsp (15 mL) pine nuts

**1**  Preheat oven to 350°F (180°C).

**2**  In a bowl blend together Parmesan, eggs,
milk, cream, oil and flour, and season well
with salt and pepper. Add pasta and herbs
and mix well.

**3**  Grease an 8 inch (20 cm) ovenproof pie
plate and line it with 2 crossed strips of foil,
then grease the foil. Pour in pasta custard
and sprinkle pine nuts on top. Bake for
about 35 minutes, until set and golden.
4 Remove from oven and cool slightly
before lifting out, using the foil strips as
handles. Serve warm or cold.

**SERVES 4 TO 6 AS A LIGHT MEAL WITH SALAD**

*Linguine with
Mushrooms*

**≈ FRITTATAS**

*Frittatas are a great way
of using cooked pasta.
To the basic egg and
pasta mixture can be
added pieces of ham,
salami, mushrooms or
cheese. Even leftover
pasta with sauce can be
used, provided the sauce
isn't too runny.*

*Penne Parcels*

# PENNE PARCELS

**½ lb (225 g) penne**

**1 tbsp (15 mL) olive oil**

**2 onions, thinly sliced**

**4 red peppers, cut into thin strips**

**5 small tomatoes, cut into thin wedges**

**1¼ inch (3 cm) sprig fresh rosemary**

**salt and freshly ground black pepper**

**2 small zucchini, julienned**

**½ cup (125 mL) chicken stock**

**1** Preheat oven to 375°F (190°C).

**2** Cook pasta in boiling salted water and drain a minute or two before it's done.

**3** Heat oil in a large frying pan and sauté onions and peppers until onions are soft and golden, 10 to 12 minutes; do not brown.

**4** Add tomatoes and rosemary and season to taste. Cook over low heat, partly covered, for 10 minutes, stirring often.

**5** Add zucchini and stock and cook for 3 to 4 minutes more, or until there is about ¼ cup (60 mL) liquid left. Remove rosemary and check seasoning. Pour sauce over penne and stir.

**6** Cut four large sheets of aluminium foil, about 12 inches square (30 cm square), and divide the pasta mixture between them. Fold each piece of foil to make a parcel and fold seams tightly so that no steam can escape. Place the bundles in a shallow baking dish and bake for 15 minutes. Serve immediately, being careful of escaping steam when opening the parcels.

### SERVES 4

### ≈ PASTA PARCELS

*Baking pasta and its sauce in a parcel expands the flavors and traps moisture, keeping the dish succulent. Many pasta-based dishes can be cooked this way. Slightly undercook the pasta initially, leaving enough liquid in the sauce for the food to steam. Seal the parcels well.*

# PASTA PIE

### BASE

**6 oz (170 g) vermicelli**

**1 tbsp (15 mL) oil**

**2 eggs, lightly beaten**

**large pinch ground nutmeg**

**3 tbsp (45 mL) finely grated fresh
Parmesan cheese**

**salt and freshly ground black pepper**

### FILLING

**½ cup (125 mL) olive oil**

**1 clove garlic, crushed**

**3⅓ cups (835 mL) canned Italian
peeled tomatoes**

**grated rind of ½ large orange**

**1 tbsp (15 mL) finely chopped fresh mint**

**large pinch sugar**

**¼ lb (110 g) fontina or Bel Paese cheese,
cut into small cubes**

**1** Preheat oven to 375°F (190°C).

**2 TO PREPARE BASE:** Cook vermicelli in boiling salted water until *al dente*. Drain. Add 1 tbsp (15 mL) olive oil and stir.

**3** In a large bowl combine eggs, nutmeg and Parmesan and season with salt and pepper. Add vermicelli and stir well to coat pasta evenly with egg mixture.

**4** Grease a 9 inch (22 cm) pie plate and press the pasta evenly over the bottom and up the sides far enough to form a shallow rim.

**5** Cover the rim loosely with a strip of foil and bake for 10 minutes, or until set. Don't remove the foil. Leave oven on.

**6 TO PREPARE FILLING:** Heat oil in a frying pan and gently sauté garlic for 1 minute. Drain tomatoes, reserving juice, and break them up with a wooden spoon before adding to the pan. Cook over low heat for 5 minutes, stirring occasionally. Add salt and pepper to taste, ⅓ cup (85 mL) of reserved tomato juice and the orange rind. Simmer until tomatoes are pulpy and thick, stirring from time to time. The mixture should be quite thick, with no excess liquid.

**7** Remove from heat and stir in mint and sugar, then let cool slightly. Stir the cheese into the tomato mixture, then spoon it into the pasta base.

**8** Bake until set, about 30 minutes. Cool slightly before serving.

**SERVES 6**

# PAPPARDELLE WITH SALAMI

**2 tsp (10 mL) olive oil**

**1 tsp (5 mL) butter**

**½ small onion, finely chopped**

**1 clove garlic, crushed**

**¼ lb (110 g) salami, thinly sliced and
cut into strips**

**½ cup (125 mL) dry white wine**

**1⅔ cups (415 mL) canned Italian peeled
tomatoes, drained**

**1 red pepper, chopped**

**1 tbsp (15 mL) raisins**

**1 tbsp (15 mL) pine nuts**

**salt and freshly ground black pepper**

**pinch each ground nutmeg and sugar**

**½ cup (125 mL) cream**

**1 lb (450 g) pappardelle**

**½ tsp (2.5 mL) chopped fresh mint**

**1 tbsp (15 mL) freshly grated
Parmesan cheese**

**1** Melt oil and butter in a large saucepan and gently sauté onion and garlic for 5 minutes. Add salami and wine and cook over high heat until wine has evaporated.

**2** Squeeze seeds and juice from tomatoes, leaving a very dry pulp. Add this to the pan, then add pepper, raisins and pine nuts. Season to taste and stir in nutmeg and sugar. Reduce heat and cook, covered, for 15 to 20 minutes. Add cream and stir.

**3** Meanwhile, put pappardelle on to cook in boiling salted water. When *al dente*, drain and add to the saucepan with mint. Toss to coat, stir in Parmesan and transfer to a warm serving dish. Serve with extra Parmesan.

**SERVES 4**

≈ **PASTA PIE BASES**

*Pasta pie bases are an interesting way of using cooked ribbon pastas. Smaller nests for individual servings are also attractive; these look good with chopped parsley or perhaps poppy seeds stirred into the pasta mixture before baking.*

≈ **PAPPARDELLE
WITH SALAMI**

*A sauce with a sweet intense flavor, this can be made lighter by omitting the salami and keeping the proportions of the other ingredients the same.*

# ROTELLI WITH TOMATOES AND GREEN OLIVES

**9 or 10 ripe tomatoes, peeled, seeded and cut into chunks**

**⅔ cup (165 mL) pitted green olives, sliced**

**2 cloves garlic, crushed**

**¼ cup (60 mL) finely chopped fresh parsley or basil, or a mixture**

**salt and freshly ground black pepper**

**½ cup (125 mL) extra virgin olive oil**

**2 to 3 drops balsamic vinegar**

**¾ lb (340 g) fresh rotelli or ⅔ lb (300 g) dried**

**1** Combine tomatoes, olives, garlic, herbs, salt and pepper in a large serving bowl. Add olive oil and vinegar and toss to coat well. Cover and let stand at room temperature for at least 2 hours to allow the flavors to develop.

**2** Cook rotelli in boiling salted water until *al dente*; drain, add to sauce and toss immediately before serving.

**SERVES 4**

# RIGATONI WITH RICOTTA

**⅔ lb (300 g) rigatoni or other large hollow tubes**

**vegetable oil**

**⅓ cup (85 mL) unsalted butter, melted**

**freshly grated Parmesan cheese**

**fresh sage or mint leaves**

**FILLING**

**⅔ lb (300 g) dry ricotta cheese**

**¾ cup (185 mL) freshly grated Parmesan cheese**

**salt and nutmeg**

**1** Cook rigatoni in boiling salted water until *al dente*; drain and stir in a little vegetable oil. Cool slightly.

**2** Preheat oven to 375°F (190°C).

**3 TO PREPARE FILLING:** In a bowl combine ricotta and Parmesan. Add salt and nutmeg to taste. Using a cake decorating bag with a ½–¾ inch (1–2 cm) nozzle, stuff each tube well with the ricotta filling.

**4** Place tubes in a greased, shallow ovenproof dish and pour butter over tubes evenly. Sprinkle with some Parmesan and toss in a couple of sage leaves. Bake for 15 minutes.

**5** Transfer to a warm serving plate, replace the sage leaves with fresh ones and serve.

**SERVES 4**

# SPINACH FETTUCCINE WITH ANCHOVIES

**1 lb (450 g) fresh spinach fettuccine or ⅔ lb (300 g) dried**

**ANCHOVY SAUCE**

**3 tbsp (45 mL) butter**

**3 tbsp (45 mL) olive oil**

**1 small onion, finely chopped**

**4 to 6 anchovy fillets, finely chopped**

**1 cup (250 mL) button mushrooms, sliced**

**freshly ground black pepper**

**EGG SAUCE**

**2 egg yolks**

**1 cup (250 mL) cream**

**3 tbsp (45 mL) grated Parmesan cheese**

**freshly ground black pepper**

**1 tsp (5 mL) chives cut into ½ inch (1 cm) lengths**

**1** Cook fettuccine in boiling salted water until *al dente*.

**2 TO PREPARE ANCHOVY SAUCE:** Heat butter and oil in a saucepan and gently sauté onion for 5 minutes. Add anchovies and sauté. Add mushrooms and toss to coat. Stir in 3 tbsp (45 mL) of pasta water. Season with pepper.

**3 TO PREPARE EGG SAUCE:** Beat together egg yolks, cream and Parmesan.

**4** Drain fettuccine, add to mushrooms and stir. Add egg sauce and chives. Toss until fettuccine is well coated and the sauce is heated through and slightly thickened. Serve with extra Parmesan and black pepper.

**SERVES 4**

# PENNE WITH EGGPLANT AND PECORINO

*This dish is rich and strong. You can add other vegetables such as zucchini and olives. For a lighter version using less oil, quickly toss diced eggplant in oil then put under the broiler, turning a couple of times, until browned.*

**1½ lbs (680 g) young, firm eggplant, cut in ¾ inch (2 cm) cubes**

**1 cup (250 mL) olive oil**

**2 cloves garlic, crushed**

**½ medium-size green pepper, thinly sliced**

**1⅔ cups (415 mL) canned Italian peeled tomatoes, strained and pulped**

**salt and freshly ground black pepper**

**1 lb (450 g) fresh penne or ¾ lb (340 g) dried**

**1 tbsp (15 mL) chopped fresh basil or 2 tbsp (30 mL) fresh parsley**

**½ cup (125 mL) grated pecorino cheese**

**1** Place eggplant in a large colander and sprinkle with salt. Leave for at least 30 minutes for the bitter juices to be drawn out by the salt. Squeeze off excess liquid before frying.

**2** In a large frying pan, heat some of the oil and fry eggplant in batches, adding more oil as needed. As each panful browns, remove from pan and set aside.

**3** Sauté garlic lightly for 30 seconds. Add green pepper and fry for 1 minute more, then add tomatoes. Season to taste and simmer for 10 minutes. Add eggplant and basil to the sauce and simmer for 2 minutes. Check seasoning then set aside to keep warm.

**4** Cook penne in boiling salted water until *al dente*. Drain and add to sauce with pecorino.

**SERVES 4**

≈ **USING QUALITY INGREDIENTS**

*As with many recipes where there are few ingredients, the quality of the ingredients makes the difference between a mediocre dish and an exceptional one. Choose the best Parmesan available, and grate it just before use.*

# PENNE WITH LEEKS, SPINACH AND PIMIENTOS

*Mellow but fresh-flavored, this dish can be served as a first course or for a light luncheon followed by cheese and fruit. It is inexpensive, easy and can be made more glamorous simply by adding sliced prosciutto, shrimp or perhaps sautéed fresh tuna.*

**3 large leeks, trimmed**

**¾ lb (340 g) fresh spinach**

**¼ cup (60 mL) butter**

**1 small onion, finely chopped**

**salt and freshly ground black pepper**

**½ large pimiento, approximately 3¼ x 1½ inches (8 x 4 cm), cut into thin strips**

**⅔ lb (300 g) penne**

**freshly grated Parmesan cheese**

**1** Slice leeks thinly, using all the whites and most of the greens. Discard spinach stalks and slice leaves thinly.

**2** Heat butter in a large pan and gently sauté onion for 4 to 5 minutes. Add leeks and spinach, season well, then cook over low heat for 10 to 15 minutes. Add the pimiento so it can cook for the last 5 minutes. Adjust seasoning to taste.

**3** Cook penne in boiling salted water until *al dente*. Drain and transfer to a warm bowl. Top with the vegetable sauce and a sprinkling of Parmesan. Serve with extra Parmesan.

**SERVES 4**

*Penne with Leeks, Spinach and Pimientos*

# MUSHROOM AND SPINACH LASAGNA

**9 dried spinach lasagna sheets, or fresh spinach pasta as follows**

### SPINACH LASAGNA

½ lb (225 g) frozen spinach, thawed

**2 eggs**

2½ cups (625 mL) all-purpose flour or 1½ cups (375 mL) all-purpose flour and ½ cup (125 mL) semolina

½ tsp (2.5 mL) salt

pinch each white pepper and ground nutmeg

### SAUCE

¼ cup (60 mL) butter

1 lb (450 g) button mushrooms, thinly sliced

**2 cloves garlic, crushed**

¼ tsp (1 mL) ground nutmeg

salt and freshly ground black pepper

1 tsp (5 mL) fresh lemon juice

¼ cup (60 mL) all-purpose flour

**3 cups (750 mL) milk**

### RICOTTA MIXTURE

2 cups (500 mL) ricotta cheese

1 small egg, beaten

¼ cup (60 mL) finely chopped fresh parsley

⅔ cup (165 mL) grated Parmesan cheese

½ lb (225 g) mozzarella cheese, shredded

**1 TO PREPARE SPINACH LASAGNA:** Put spinach in a tea towel and wring it out thoroughly to remove all excess water. Purée in a food processor or blender with 1 egg.

**2** Stir flour(s) and seasonings together, then form a well in the center. Break the second egg into the well and beat it with a fork for seven or eight strokes before beginning to incorporate the flour. Mix until the mixture becomes dry, then add puréed spinach and work this into the flour. Continue until dough becomes sticky and difficult to work with the fork, then begin to knead by hand using extra flour as needed to form a smooth and elastic ball. Let dough rest for

at least 20 minutes. This whole step can be done in a food processor if preferred.

**3** Divide dough into three or four balls and cover them with plastic wrap or a tea towel. Roll each ball into an even thin sheet, using a hand-cranked pasta machine or by hand with a rolling pin. Let the sheets rest before trimming them into workable sizes for cooking.

**4** In a large pan of boiling salted water cook the lasagna sheets in batches for 1 minute. Remove with a slotted spoon and drain on tea towels before proceeding. If using dried pasta, cook according to the directions on the package. Drain as above.

**5** Preheat oven to 350°F (180°C).

**6 TO PREPARE SAUCE:** Melt butter in a large saucepan and add mushrooms, garlic, nutmeg, salt and pepper. Stir, then add lemon juice. Sauté for 2 to 3 minutes; do not brown. Stir in flour, cook for half a minute, then slowly add milk. Cook, stirring, until thickened into a smooth sauce.

**7 TO PREPARE RICOTTA MIXTURE:** In a small bowl combine ricotta, egg, half the parsley and most of the Parmesan.

**8** Grease a large ovenproof dish and line it with some of the pasta sheets, bringing them up the sides and letting them fall over the rim; this will form an outer case for the lasagna. Cover with one-third of the ricotta mixture, one-third of the mozzarella and one-third of the mushroom sauce. Put in another layer of pasta, just as wide as the dish this time, and continue the sequence of layering, ending with the last of the mushroom sauce on top. Sprinkle with the remaining parsley and Parmesan. Now fold over the pasta flaps and trim, if necessary, so that they form a ¾ – 1¼ inch (2 – 3 cm) border around the lasagna.

**9** Cover the dish loosely with foil and bake for 40 minutes or so. Let stand in a warm spot for 10 minutes before serving.

**SERVES 8**

≈ **MUSHROOM AND SPINACH LASAGNA**

*This lasagna is surprisingly light and makes an excellent luncheon or late supper dish. It can be prepared beforehand and isn't as time-consuming as other lasagnas, particularly if you are able to purchase the spinach pasta sheets. It can be made using plain pasta, but the subtle mix of flavors is lessened, along with some of the visual appeal.*

*A fresh tomato sauce accompanies this cake beautifully. It is also easy to convert to a more substantial meal by introducing layers of stir-fried vegetables, salami or ham. It keeps well and tastes equally delicious served cold.*

# MACARONI, CHEESE AND EGG CAKE

**1 lb (450 g) elbow macaroni or ziti**

### CHEESE SAUCE

**2 tbsp (30 mL) butter**
**3 tbsp (45 mL) all-purpose flour**
**2½ cups (625 mL) milk**
**salt, white pepper and nutmeg**
**1⅓ cups (335 mL) grated Cheddar cheese**
**2 tbsp (30 mL) grated Parmesan cheese**
**1 tsp (5 mL) grated onion**
**2 tsp (10 mL) Dijon-style mustard**
**1½ tsp (7.5 mL) chopped fresh parsley**

### CRUST

**5 tbsp (75 mL) grated Parmesan cheese**
**5 tbsp (75 mL) bread crumbs**
**1 egg, beaten**
**½ lb (225 g) mozzarella cheese, grated**
**3 hard-boiled eggs, shelled and sliced**

**1** Cook macaroni in boiling salted water until *al dente*. Drain and stir in a little vegetable oil to prevent sticking.

**2 TO PREPARE CHEESE SAUCE:** In a small saucepan melt butter and stir in flour. Cook until smooth. Gradually stir in the milk. Cook, stirring, until sauce begins to thicken. Add salt, pepper and nutmeg to taste, Cheddar, Parmesan, onion, mustard and parsley. Continue to cook until thick and smooth. In a bowl combine pasta with cheese sauce and mix well.

**3** Preheat oven to 350°F (180°C).

**4 TO PREPARE CRUST:** Mix Parmesan and bread crumbs together and sprinkle some in a greased deep-sided rectangular casserole. Shake them around to coat the walls well, then shake out the excess. Pour in egg and swirl around the dish to cover bread crumb mixture. Discard excess, then shake around a final coating of bread crumbs and Parmesan.

**5** Layer one-third of the pasta in the bottom of the dish. Cover with one-third of the mozzarella. Place half the boiled egg slices in a single layer on top. Repeat layering. On the last level of eggs put the remaining pasta and finally the last of the mozzarella.

**6** Bake for 20 to 30 minutes. Allow the cake to cool for 15 minutes, and then run a sharp knife around the edge to loosen it. Carefully turn out onto a warm serving plate and serve in slices.

**SERVES 6 TO 8**

*Bottled or canned clams work very well here, and the sauce is just as good if you'd like to leave out the mushrooms. Or you can use snails instead of clams.*

# LINGUINE IN WHITE CLAM SAUCE

**10 oz (300 g) baby clams in brine, bottled or canned**
**1 cup (250 mL) milk**
**3 tbsp (45 mL) olive oil**
**2 tbsp (30 mL) butter**
**1 clove garlic, crushed**
**1 small onion, finely chopped**
**1¼ cups (310 mL) button mushrooms, sliced**
**½ cup (125 mL) dry white wine**
**1 tbsp (15 mL) finely chopped fresh parsley**
**2 tsp (10 mL) finely chopped fresh basil**
**1 tsp (5 mL) finely chopped fresh oregano or ¼ tsp (1 mL) dried**
**salt and white pepper**
**1 lb (450 g) fresh linguine or ⅔ lb (300 g) dried**
**4 sprigs fresh basil, to garnish**

**1** Drain clams and soak in milk for 1 to 1½ hours. Drain again, reserving ½ cup (125 mL) of the liquid.

**2** Heat oil and butter in a large pot and gently sauté garlic and onion until soft. Add mushrooms, sauté briefly, and then pour in wine. Cook over medium heat to reduce slightly, then add the herbs, clams and clam milk. Season well and cook until the sauce thickens somewhat.

**3** Cook linguine in boiling salted water until *al dente*. Drain and transfer to a heated serving dish. Pour on the sauce and decorate with sprigs of basil.

**SERVES 4**

# PUMPKIN GNOCCHI

**2 lbs (1 kg) pumpkin, skin left on**
**⅓ cup (85 mL) semolina**
**⅓ – ⅔ cup (85 – 165 mL) potato flour**
**salt, white pepper and ground nutmeg**
**¼ lb (110 g) unsalted butter**
**freshly grated Parmesan cheese**

**1** Preheat oven to 350°F (180°C).

**2** Cut pumpkin into pieces. Place in a shallow baking dish, skin side up, pour in ¼ cup (60 mL) water and bake until tender.

**3** Remove from the oven and cool. Peel off the skin and any burnt surfaces, then mash the flesh or put it through a food mill to yield 2 cups (500 mL) pulp. (It's not recommended to use a blender or food processor, as the resulting purée tends to be watery and lack body.)

**4** Put pumpkin in a large bowl, season and begin to work in the flours. Use all the semolina and as much of the potato flour as you need to make a soft kneadable dough. Add salt, pepper and nutmeg. Knead lightly until elastic. Let rest for 10 minutes.

**5** Break off little pieces about ¾ inch (2 cm) long. Roll them quickly between your fingers to obtain a smoother surface, then press them with your thumb against the curved back of a fork or grater to get the traditional gnocchi shape. Dust lightly with potato flour and let rest for 10 to 12 minutes.

**6** Melt butter in a saucepan and cook over medium heat until golden brown. Keep warm.

**7** Cook the gnocchi, a few at a time, in boiling salted water. When they rise to the surface remove with a slotted spoon and transfer to warm bowls. Pour the butter over the top, sprinkle on some Parmesan and serve immediately. Extra Parmesan can be served separately.

**SERVES 4**

≈ **PUMPKIN GNOCCHI**

*Choose firm, richly colored pumpkin for good texture and flavor, and work quickly and lightly with the dough to avoid toughness. If you are busy it is possible to boil the pumpkin instead of baking it, but the flavor won't be as intense, or the texture as firm.*

*Preparing Pumpkin Gnocchi with brown butter and Parmesan*

# SPINACH CHIPS

**1 lb (450 g) frozen spinach, thawed**

**1⅔ cups (415 mL) semolina**

**2 eggs**

**1 tsp (5 mL) vegetable oil**

**1 tbsp (15 mL) salt**

**¼ cup (60 mL) grated Parmesan cheese**

**1 tsp (5 mL) freshly ground black pepper**

**1 tsp (5 mL) dried oregano**

**1 tsp (5 mL) onion salt**

**1 tsp (5 mL) garlic salt**

**vegetable oil for frying**

*Spinach Chips*

**1** Put spinach in a tea towel and wring it thoroughly dry. Blend in a food processor with all the remaining ingredients except frying oil. Blend until a smooth ball of dough forms and stops the machine. If mixing by hand, chop spinach finely first.

**2** Knead dough (incorporating some flour if necessary to give a dry but pliable consistency) until smooth and elastic, about 6 minutes. Cover with a damp cloth or plastic wrap and let stand for 30 minutes.

**3** Divide the ball into four pieces and roll each piece out very thinly, using a rolling pin or pasta machine. Sprinkle each sheet lightly with flour and let stand for 15 minutes more. Using a sharp knife or a pastry cutting wheel, cut the sheets into rectangles of about 2 by ¾ inches (5 by 2 cm).

**4** Heat frying oil to 365°F (185°C), or until a slight haze is visible. Toss in one or two chips to check that the temperature is right, then fry them quickly in batches. It should take 5 to 10 seconds if deep-frying, or 5 to 8 seconds each side if shallow-frying. Remove with a slotted spoon and drain on paper towels before cooling.

**MAKES ABOUT 100**

# RICOTTA AND SALAMI IN WINE PASTA

### PASTA

2½ cups (625 mL) all-purpose flour
large pinch salt
large pinch sugar
1 egg, beaten
½ cup (125 mL) dry white wine,
or more if needed

### FILLING

1 cup (250 mL) ricotta cheese
1 egg
¼ lb (110 g) smoked mozzarella,
finely diced
2½ oz (70 g) lean salami, finely diced
1 tbsp (15 mL) grated Parmesan cheese
¼ tsp (1 mL) freshly ground black pepper
3 tbsp (45 mL) dried bread crumbs
1 tbsp (15 mL) finely chopped fresh mint
beaten egg for sealing
vegetable oil for frying

**1 TO PREPARE PASTA:** Pile flour, salt and sugar on a work surface and make a well in the center. Add egg and wine, and begin incorporating dry ingredients with a fork. When a rough dough is formed, begin kneading, adding more flour or wine to make it pliable but dry to the touch. Knead for at least 6 minutes, or until smooth and elastic. Cover with a damp cloth or plastic wrap and let stand for 30 minutes. Divide into three pieces and roll each piece out to a very thin sheet. Cover and let rest for 15 minutes before cutting.

**2 TO PREPARE FILLING:** Combine all ingredients in a bowl and mix well.

**3** Cut pasta circles 4–5 inches (10–12 cm) in diameter. Paint the rim of each circle with egg, then place 2 tsp (10 mL) filling along the center. Fold over to form a half-moon shape and press edges together. Cut around the rims with a zigzag pastry wheel or a crimper cutter and set aside in a single layer until ready to cook.

**4** Heat vegetable oil for deep-frying until a slight haze is visible. Fry pastries, two or three at a time, until golden and crisp on both sides. Remove with a slotted spoon and drain on paper towels before serving.

**SERVES 3 TO 4**

# HAM AND MUSHROOM LASAGNA

3 tbsp (45 mL) olive oil
1 small onion, finely chopped
3¼ cups (810 mL) button mushrooms, sliced
3⅓ cups (835 mL) canned Italian peeled
tomatoes, drained and finely chopped
¼ cup (60 mL) chopped fresh parsley
dry white wine
salt and freshly ground black pepper
1 lb (450 g) fresh lasagna sheets or
⅔ lb (300 g) packaged lasagna
toasted fresh bread crumbs
12 oz (340 g) unsmoked ham, cut into strips
8 oz (225 g) mozzarella, shredded
2 hard-boiled eggs, thinly sliced

**1** In a large pan heat oil and gently sauté onion until soft. Add mushrooms and sauté briefly. Add tomatoes and parsley. Cook, covered, for 40 minutes, adding a little wine if the sauce becomes dry. Season lightly.

**2** Cook the lasagna sheets, a few at a time, in boiling salted water until *al dente*. Remove with a large flat slotted spoon or a skimmer and place on dry tea towels to drain.

**3** Preheat oven to 375°F (190°C).

**4** Grease a deep rectangular ovenproof dish and toss bread crumbs in it to coat the sides. Discard any surplus.

**5** Place a layer of pasta over the bottom and right up the sides. Spoon in one-third of the sauce, cover with a layer of ham, then one-third of the mozzarella, then layer half the egg slices on top. Cover these with a layer of pasta, half the remaining sauce, and continue the layers until the last is the remaining mozzarella. Fold over the top any pasta from the sides that may be exposed.

**6** Bake for 30 minutes. Let sit for 3 to 4 minutes in a warm spot before serving.

**SERVES 4 TO 6**

≋ WINE PASTA

*Pasta made with white wine and a touch of sugar has a flavor reminiscent of yeast dough. If the sugar is left out, the pasta, cut into shapes or ribbons, can be served with a sauce. You can substitute Bruder Basil cheese for the smoked mozzarella in this recipe.*

≋ HAM AND MUSHROOM LASAGNA

*This deep-flavored lasagna can be served as an entrée or as the main course. Made without a white sauce, it makes a less rich dish than other lasagna, and eliminates a time-consuming step. It can be prepared up to 24 hours in advance and kept in the refrigerator until needed.*

# FAST PASTA

This is what pasta is all about in today's kitchen: a filling meal ready in the time it takes to cook the fettuccine or spaghetti, and one you have prepared yourself, easily and without fuss. Because the cooking time is brief, the nutritional content of the ingredients is not lost and there's the added bonus that often there is very little washing up.

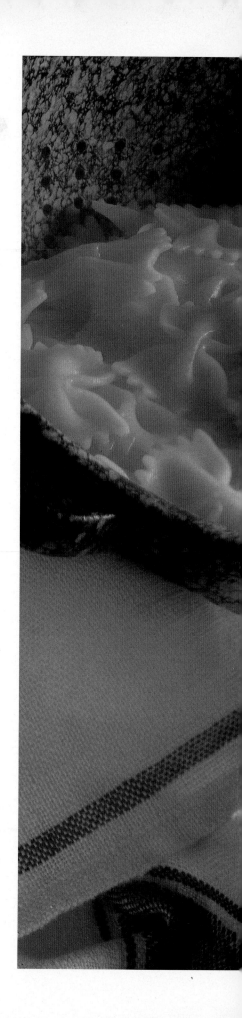

## TOMATO TAGLIERINI WITH FENNEL SAUCE

**2 large fennel bulbs**

**1 lb (450 g) fresh tomato taglierini**

**¼ cup (60 mL) butter**

**¼ cup (60 mL) olive oil**

**1 clove garlic, crushed**

**½ cup (125 mL) dry white wine**

**3¼ cups (810 mL) button mushrooms, sliced**

**salt and white pepper**

**⅓ cup (85 mL) cream**

**2 tsp (10 mL) finely chopped fresh parsley**

**3 tbsp (45 mL) coarsely grated Parmesan cheese**

**1** Trim fennel bulbs and parboil them. Discard any tough outer stalks, then slice bulbs thinly.

**2** Cook taglierini in boiling salted water until *al dente.*

**3** Heat butter and oil together in a frying pan and stir in garlic. Add fennel and white wine. Cook for 1 to 2 minutes, then add mushrooms and season with salt and pepper to taste. Cook 3 minutes. Add cream and parsley and cook for 30 seconds more. Stir in Parmesan.

**4** Stir sauce into cooked and drained pasta and serve with extra grated Parmesan.

**SERVES 4**

# GORGONZOLA AND PISTACHIO FETTUCCINE

*The secret of this recipe is to move quickly once the Gorgonzola has been added, to keep the cheese from separating.*

½ lb (225 g) dried fettuccine or
¾ lb (340 g) fresh

2 tbsp (30 mL) butter

3 tbsp (45 mL) olive oil

1 clove garlic

3 tbsp (45 mL) finely chopped fresh parsley

2 oz (60 g) shelled pistachio nuts

¼ lb (110 g) milk Gorgonzola or other
creamy blue cheese, e.g. Castello

3 tbsp (45 mL) grated Parmesan cheese

**1** Cook the fettuccine in boiling salted water until *al dente*.

**2** Heat butter and oil in a pan and sauté garlic. Stir in parsley and pistachios. Cook, stirring, for 2 minutes. Remove garlic clove. Add crumbled blue cheese and stir until melted. Mix 3 tbsp (45 mL) pasta water into the sauce.

**3** When pasta is cooked, drain. Add sauce and Parmesan to fettuccine and stir. Serve with extra grated Parmesan.

**SERVES 4 AS AN ENTRÉE**

# TORTELLINI VERDI WITH RICOTTA AND PISTACHIO NUTS

1 lb (450 g) spinach tortellini with
ricotta filling

½ cup (125 mL) ricotta cheese

¼ cup (60 mL) grated Parmesan cheese

3 tbsp (45 mL) cream

2 eggs

salt and white pepper

12 pistachio nuts, shelled and roughly
chopped

*Ingredients for Gorgonzola and Pistachio Fettuccine*

**1** Begin cooking tortellini.

**2** In a blender or food processor combine ricotta, Parmesan and cream and mix until smooth. Transfer to a saucepan and set over a pot of boiling water. Stir occasionally while heating.

**3** Beat eggs with salt and pepper to taste.

**4** When tortellini are cooked, drain and quickly toss with the egg mixture and the sauce. Decorate with pistachios and serve with extra grated Parmesan.

**SERVES 6 AS AN ENTRÉE**

# CONCHIGLIE WITH SPINACH AND ALMOND SAUCE

½ lb (225 g) small dried conchiglie
or ¾ lb (340 g) fresh

½ lb (225 g) cooked drained spinach,
fresh or frozen

1 tbsp (15 mL) chopped fresh basil
or 1 tsp (5 mL) dried

⅓ cup plus 1 tbsp (100 mL) roughly
chopped fresh parsley

1 cup (250 mL) grated pecorino cheese

½ cup (125 mL) blanched almonds

2 cloves garlic, chopped

¼ cup (60 mL) butter, softened

¼ cup (60 mL) extra virgin olive oil

extra grated pecorino or grated pepato,
to serve

**1** Cook conchiglie in boiling salted water until *al dente*.

**2** Place all remaining ingredients in a blender or food processor and blend to a smooth paste. Take 5 tbsp (75 mL) of the pasta cooking water and blend into the sauce.

**3** Drain cooked pasta, add sauce and stir. Serve with extra grated pecorino, or use grated pepato for added oomph.

**SERVES 4 AS AN ENTRÉE OR LIGHT MEAL**

≈ **SPINACH AND ALMOND SAUCE**
*The beautiful color and good coating quality of this sauce make it very versatile. You can toss in some diced feta cheese or some crisp bacon pieces, or serve the dish in smaller portions as an accompaniment to broiled or poached fish.*

# ZUCCHINI WITH SAFFRON SAUCE

1 lb (450 g) penne or orecchiette

3 tbsp (45 mL) vegetable oil

2 cloves garlic, crushed

1⅓ lbs (600 g) small young zucchini, cut into ¼ inch (0.5 cm) slices

salt, pepper and nutmeg

⅔ cup (165 mL) cream

½ tsp (2.5 mL) pure saffron powder or ¼ tsp (1 mL) saffron strands

grated Parmesan cheese, to serve

**1**  Cook penne in boiling salted water until *al dente*.

**2**  Heat oil in a large frying pan and sauté garlic and zucchini until golden brown but still crisp. Add salt, pepper and nutmeg to taste.

**3**  Meanwhile bring cream and saffron to the boil. Simmer gently until cream is slightly thickened and a mellow saffron color.

**4**  Reserve a few slices of zucchini for decoration. Drain cooked pasta and add to the zucchini pan with saffron cream. Stir to coat well.

**5**  Garnish with reserved zucchini. Serve grated Parmesan separately.

**SERVES 4 AS A MAIN COURSE**

# SPAGHETTINI WITH ZUCCHINI AND WALNUTS

1 lb (450 g) fresh spaghettini or ⅔ lb (300 g) dried

¼ cup (60 mL) olive oil

½ small onion, finely chopped

1 clove garlic, crushed

1 cup (250 mL) chopped walnuts

4 small zucchini, grated

3 tbsp (45 mL) finely chopped fresh parsley

2 tsp (10 mL) chopped fresh basil or ½ tsp (2.5 mL) dried

salt and freshly ground black pepper

pinch nutmeg

⅓ cup (85 mL) butter

¼ cup (60 mL) freshly grated Parmesan cheese

**1**  Begin cooking spaghettini in boiling salted water.

**2**  Heat oil in a large frying pan and gently sauté onion and garlic until soft. Add walnuts and sauté until slightly colored.

**3**  Add zucchini, parsley and basil and cook, stirring, for 20 seconds. Season to taste with salt, pepper and nutmeg. Add butter and cook until butter is bubbling.

**4**  When pasta is *al dente*, drain and add to sauce. Add Parmesan and toss to coat before serving.

**SERVES 4 AS AN ENTRÉE**

# FETTUCCINE WITH RICOTTA AND DILL SAUCE

1 lb (450 g) fresh whole-wheat fettuccine or ⅔ lb (300 g) dried

1 clove garlic, crushed

2 cups (500 mL) ricotta cheese

1½ cups (375 mL) milk

1½ tsp (7.5 mL) salt

pinch each white pepper and cayenne pepper

pinch chili powder

½ red pepper, chopped

3 tbsp (45 mL) chopped fresh dill

**1**  Cook fettuccine in boiling salted water until *al dente*.

**2**  In a blender or food processor blend garlic, ricotta, milk, salt, peppers and chili to form a smooth sauce. Transfer to a bowl and stir in pepper and dill.

**3**  When pasta is *al dente*, mix 1–3 tbsp (15–45 mL) cooking water through the sauce, then drain pasta. Add sauce to pasta and stir to coat before serving.

**SERVES 4**

# VERMICELLI WITH WALNUT SAUCE

*This dish goes very well before a main course of fish or poultry. The rich, crunchy sauce keeps well in the refrigerator for up to 4 days, and it is also good served as a dip with crudités.*

**¾ lb (340 g) fresh vermicelli or ½ lb (225 g) dried**

**1¼ cups (325 mL) walnut halves**

**2 cups (500 mL) roughly chopped fresh parsley**

**5 tbsp (75 mL) fresh or dried bread crumbs**

**6 tbsp (90 mL) butter, softened**

**½ cup (125 mL) extra virgin olive oil**

**¼ cup (60 mL) cream**

**salt and white pepper**

**1** Begin cooking pasta in boiling salted water.

**2** Place walnuts, parsley and bread crumbs in a food processor or blender and chop until finely ground. Add butter and oil and blend again to form a thick green paste.

**3** Add cream and season to taste with salt and pepper. Blend to combine.

**4** Drain cooked pasta and transfer to a warm serving dish. Stir in sauce and serve immediately. This dish is usually served without cheese.

**SERVES 4 AS AN ENTRÉE**

*Walnut Sauce*

# GNOCCHI WITH FONTINA SAUCE

**7 oz (200 g) fontina cheese, grated or finely chopped**

**½ cup (125 mL) cream**

**⅓ cup (85 mL) butter**

**¼ cup (60 mL) grated Parmesan cheese**

**1 lb (450 g) gnocchi dumplings**

**few leaves fresh sage, to garnish**

**1** Place fontina, cream, butter and Parmesan in a bowl or saucepan over another saucepan of simmering water. Heat, stirring occasionally, until the cheeses have melted and the sauce is smooth and hot.

**2** In the meantime start boiling water for the gnocchi, and when the sauce is about halfway done, put in the gnocchi. Drain cooked gnocchi and coat with a little vegetable oil.

**3** Serve with sauce poured over gnocchi. Garnish with sage leaves sprinkled on top.

**SERVES 4**

# BAKED PASTA WITH ZUCCHINI AND MOZZARELLA

**⅔ lb (300 g) shaped pasta (fusilli, orecchiette or conchiglie)**

**¼ cup (60 mL) olive oil**

**5 small young zucchini, cut into ½ inch (1 cm) slices**

**salt and freshly ground black pepper**

**1⅔ cups (415 mL) canned Italian peeled tomatoes, drained and pulped**

**8 to 10 black olives, pitted and sliced**

**3 tbsp (45 mL) freshly grated Parmesan cheese**

**1 tsp (5 mL) fresh rosemary sprigs**

**½ lb (225 g) mozzarella cheese, cut into ½ inch (1 cm) cubes**

*Gnocchi with Fontina Sauce*

**1** Cook pasta in boiling salted water.

**2** In a large frying pan, heat oil and sauté zucchini until lightly browned, about 5 minutes. Season with salt and pepper and transfer to an oiled shallow casserole dish.

**3** Preheat oven to 350°F (180°C).

**4** When pasta is almost cooked, drain and add to zucchini. Add tomatoes, olives, Parmesan, rosemary and one-third of the mozzarella. Sprinkle with a little more salt and pepper if desired, then toss gently.

**5** Cover with remaining mozzarella and bake until cheese is melted and the top slightly browned, about 15 minutes.

**SERVES 4**

# TAGLIERINI WITH SUN-DRIED TOMATOES AND SNOW PEAS

**¾ lb (340 g) fresh taglierini or ½ lb (225 g) dried**

**⅓ cup (85 mL) extra virgin olive oil**

**3 or 4 cloves garlic, crushed**

**1 tbsp (15 mL) finely chopped fresh mint**

**1 tbsp (15 mL) finely chopped fresh parsley**

**12 to 15 small snow peas, sliced diagonally into three**

**10 to 12 oil-packed sun-dried tomatoes, rinsed, drained and sliced thinly**

**juice of ½ lemon**

**salt and freshly ground black pepper**

**1** Begin cooking taglierini in boiling salted water.

**2** Heat oil and very gently sauté garlic and herbs for 1 to 2 minutes. Keep heat low enough so that oil does not splatter. Add snow peas and toss for 1 minute, then stir in sun-dried tomatoes. Add lemon juice and season to taste with salt and pepper.

**3** Drain cooked taglierini and stir it into the pan with the vegetables. Toss well.

**SERVES 4**

≈ **GNOCCHI WITH FONTINA SAUCE**

*Fresh sage and cheese have an affinity that gives a subtle flavor hard to duplicate with dried sage. So if fresh sage is not available, try adding a different flavor, such as julienned red peppers or thin strips of oil-packed sun-dried tomatoes. Stir into the sauce just before serving.*

≈ **TAGLIERINI WITH SUN-DRIED TOMATOES AND SNOW PEAS**

*There is no substitute for sun-dried tomatoes. If you can buy only packaged sun-dried tomatoes, plump them in hot water before using. If unavailable, leave them out of the recipe. It will, of course, taste different.*

# TUNA, OLIVE AND CAPER SAUCE

14 oz (375 g) canned tuna in brine

3 tbsp (45 mL) butter

3 tbsp (45 mL) all-purpose flour

1 cup (250 mL) milk

salt and white pepper

2 tsp (10 mL) chopped fresh parsley

2 tsp (10 mL) chopped fresh chives

juice of ½ lemon

12 black olives, pitted and sliced

2 tsp (10 mL) small capers (or large capers, chopped)

4 to 5 drops Tabasco sauce

**1** Drain tuna and reserve brine. Melt butter in a large saucepan and add flour. Cook, stirring, until smooth and golden. Add milk and reserved brine and gradually stir to a thick, smooth sauce.

**2** Season to taste with salt and pepper and stir in parsley and chives. Add lemon juice, olives, capers and Tabasco sauce; stir well. Break up tuna into small chunks and add to sauce; heat through.

**SERVES 4**

## ≈ BUYING AND USING SCALLOPS

*Scallops should have creamy white meat and roe intact. They should be firm with a pleasant smell. If buying them in the shell, shells should be closed. Scallop meat can be stored in the refrigerator for up to 3 days in an airtight container. Before cooking, remove the brown vein. You don't need to remove the roe.*

# TAGLIATELLE WITH SCALLOPS AND SMOKED SALMON

3 tbsp (45 mL) unsalted butter

1 clove garlic, crushed

1 tbsp (15 mL) grated onion

16 small scallops, cleaned and soaked in milk for 30 minutes

1 lb (450 g) fresh tagliatelle or ⅔ lb (300 g) dried

⅔ cup (165 mL) dry white wine

2 tsp (10 mL) finely chopped fresh parsley

salt and white pepper

⅔ cup (165 mL) cream

4 oz (110 g) smoked salmon, julienned

**1** Heat butter and gently sauté garlic clove and onion for 1 to 2 minutes. Add drained scallops and quickly fry until opaque.

**2** Put tagliatelle on to cook in boiling salted water.

**3** Add wine and parsley to scallops and over high heat reduce liquid by half. Season to taste, then stir in cream. Lower the heat and cook until cream begins to thicken.

**4** Drain tagliatelle when *al dente* and transfer to a warm serving dish. Pour on sauce, add smoked salmon and toss quickly before serving.

**SERVES 4 AS AN ENTRÉE**

# ROTELLI WITH SPINACH AND ANCHOVIES

¾ lb (340 g) fresh rotelli or ⅔ lb (300 g) dried

3 tbsp (45 mL) butter

3 cloves garlic, crushed

8 anchovy fillets, finely chopped

2 cups (500 mL) chopped, cooked and drained spinach, fresh or frozen

3⅓ cups (835 mL) canned Italian peeled tomatoes, drained

⅓ cup (85 mL) pine nuts, toasted

**1** Cook rotelli in boiling salted water until *al dente.*

**2** Melt butter in a large frying pan and sauté garlic gently for 30 seconds. Stir in anchovies and cook for another 30 seconds. Add spinach and cook to evaporate any remaining moisture; the mixture should be quite dry at this stage.

**3** Break up tomatoes in your hand over the sink, shaking off excess juice, and then add pulp to spinach in the pan.

**4** Drain cooked pasta lightly so that some cooking water remains, then stir pasta into spinach mixture with pine nuts. Toss well before serving. Cheese is not usually served with this dish.

**SERVES 4 AS AN ENTRÉE**

# SEAFOOD WITH FRESH TAGLIATELLE

*Very easy and very quick, this dish requires fresh pasta (preferably made from durum wheat semolina) to enable fast cooking in the final step. The result is a deliciously fresh combination of flavors.*

**⅓ cup (85 mL) olive oil**

**2 cloves garlic, crushed**

**1 lb (450 g) lobster, cut into pieces, with shells left on**

**1 lb (450 g) shrimp, shelled and deveined, with tails left on**

**⅔ lb (300 g) white fish fillets, cut into pieces**

**2 large tomatoes, peeled, seeded and chopped**

**4 oz (110 g) red pimientos, chopped**

**1 tsp (5 mL) paprika**

**½ tsp (2.5 mL) pure saffron powder**

**salt**

**4 cups (1 L) light fish stock**

**1¾ lbs (800 g) fresh egg tagliatelle**

**1** In a large frying pan heat oil and add garlic. Sauté briefly and add seafood. Cook, stirring, until well coated with garlic oil.

**2** Add tomatoes, pimientos, paprika, saffron and salt to taste. Pour in stock and bring to the boil. Add tagliatelle, stir in and simmer until *al dente*, 1 to 3 minutes. If it looks as though there will be excess juice, increase the heat for the last half minute to reduce liquid.

**3** The dish is ready when the pasta is cooked. Take the pan to the table and serve immediately.

**SERVES 6 TO 8**

*Seafood with Fresh Tagliatelle*

### ≈ PREPARING SHRIMP

*Cut off the head and remove the shell. The tail doesn't have to be removed. Use a sharp knife to slit the center and back and pull the vein out.*

# TORTELLINI WITH SAUSAGE

**1 lb (450 g) meat tortellini**

**1½ tbsp (20 mL) butter**

**½ green pepper, sliced**

**3 good quality sausages, preferably spicy, cut in ¾ inch (2 cm) pieces**

**¾ cup (185 mL) ricotta cheese**

**½ cup (125 mL) grated pecorino cheese**

**salt and freshly ground black pepper**

**1**  Cook tortellini in boiling salted water.

**2**  Melt butter and sauté pepper and sausage until sausage is browned and cooked through.

**3**  In a bowl combine ricotta and pecorino, a little salt and generous grindings of black pepper. Just before serving, beat in 1½– 2½ tbsp (20–40 mL) boiling pasta water.

**4**  Drain tortellini and transfer to a warm serving dish. Add ricotta and sausage mixtures and toss to distribute evenly.

**SERVES 4**

≈ **COOKING WITH LIVER**

*Young calf's liver can be used instead of lamb's, but either way cook only when ready to eat; reheated liver is dry, tough and sharply flavored.*

# PAPPARDELLE WITH LAMB'S LIVER AND BACON

**1 lb (450 g) fresh pappardelle or ⅔ lb (300 g) dried**

**3 tbsp (45 mL) butter**

**1 clove garlic**

**1 small onion, thinly sliced**

**¼ lb (110 g) bacon, sliced into short strips**

**1½ tsp (7.5 mL) chopped fresh sage or ½ tsp (2.5 mL) dried**

**10 oz (300 g) lamb's liver, cleaned and sliced into strips**

**¼ cup (60 mL) vermouth**

**1 tbsp (15 mL) puréed fresh tomato or the juice from a can of Italian peeled tomatoes**

**salt and freshly ground black pepper**

**1**  Begin cooking pappardelle in boiling salted water.

**2**  Melt butter in a large frying pan and gently sauté garlic clove and onion until soft; do not brown.

**3**  Add bacon and sauté until crisp, and then add sage and liver. Increase heat slightly and sauté until liver is just brown.

**4**  Remove garlic clove and add vermouth and tomato purée; reduce. Season to taste and add a little stock or extra tomato purée if sauce is too thick.

**5**  When the pasta is *al dente*, drain and stir into sauce before serving.

**SERVES 4 AS AN ENTRÉE OR LIGHT MAIN COURSE**

# LASAGNETTE WITH CHICKEN LIVERS

**½ lb (225 g) small young green beans, both ends trimmed**

**1 lb (450 g) lasagnette**

**2 tbsp (30 mL) walnut oil**

**2 tbsp (30 mL) butter**

**10 oz (300 g) chicken livers, cleaned, trimmed and cut in half**

**1¼ cups (310 mL) button mushrooms, sliced**

**1 tsp (5 mL) balsamic vinegar or 1 tbsp (15 mL) sherry vinegar**

**salt and white pepper**

**½ cup (125 mL) chicken stock**

**1 tbsp (15 mL) roughly torn fresh Italian parsley leaves**

**5 to 6 walnut halves, roughly chopped (optional)**

**1**  In a large pot of boiling water, blanch beans for 1 minute. Remove with a slotted spoon and rinse under cold water; drain. Add lasagnette to the boiling water with a pinch of salt and cook until *al dente*; drain.

**2**  Meanwhile, heat oil and butter in a large frying pan and add livers. Sauté quickly until browned on the outside but pink and juicy inside. Add mushrooms and stir, then add vinegar. Increase heat slightly and reduce liquid.

**3**  Season to taste, then pour in stock and quickly reduce by half. Toss in beans and lasagnette and stir in parsley. Serve on warm plates decorated with walnuts.

**SERVES 4**

# SMOKED TURKEY AND GNOCCHI SALAD

¼ lb (110 g) dried gnocchi shapes (not dumplings)

3 tbsp (45 mL) olive oil

8 oz (225 g) smoked turkey, flaked into pieces 1¼ – 1½ inches (3 – 4 cm) long

⅔ cup (165 mL) button mushrooms, sliced

1 tbsp (15 mL) chopped fresh chives

freshly ground black pepper

1 tsp (5 mL) balsamic vinegar

2 tsp (10 mL) extra virgin olive oil

2 small avocados or 1 large, quartered and sliced

¼ lb (110 g) natural smoked cheese (e.g. smoked mozzarella or Bruder Basil) cut into ½ inch (1 cm) cubes

**1** Cook pasta in boiling salted water until *al dente*. Drain and rinse in cold water. Drain again and set aside.

**2** Heat olive oil in a large frying pan and sauté turkey pieces, mushrooms and chives until turkey is lightly browned. Season well with black pepper. Add vinegar and olive oil and cook, stirring, until the liquid has reduced and thickened. Season again. Add pasta and toss well; cook for 10 to 15 seconds.

**3** Remove pan from heat and add avocado slices and cheese. Stir well to distribute the heat; then let the dish stand for 2 to 3 minutes before serving. Serve warm, or cool completely and serve at room temperature.

**SERVES 4 AS AN ENTRÉE**

*Smoked Turkey and Gnocchi Salad*

*Tomato Fettuccine
with Scallops*

# TOMATO FETTUCCINE
# WITH SCALLOPS

¼ lb (110 g) unsalted butter

3 cloves garlic, crushed

1¾ cups (440 mL) button mushrooms, sliced

3 tbsp (45 mL) fresh lemon juice

½ lb (225 g) fresh scallops

4 very small young zucchini,
cut into 1¼ inch (3 cm) long julienne strips

3 tbsp (45 mL) finely chopped fresh parsley

salt and freshly ground black pepper

pinch cayenne pepper

1 lb (450 g) fresh tomato fettuccine

3 tbsp (45 mL) chopped fresh parsley,
to garnish

**1** In a large frying pan melt half the butter and sauté garlic for 1 minute; do not brown.
**2** Add mushrooms and lemon juice and toss well. Add scallops with zucchini and parsley. Cover and steam gently, shaking frequently, for 1 to 2 minutes. Add remaining butter and when it's melted and blended, add salt and pepper. Add cayenne.
**3** Meanwhile, begin cooking pasta. When it is *al dente*, drain and add to sauce. Garnish with parsley.

**SERVES 4**

# PENNE WITH SHRIMP AND BACON

**1 lb (450 g) penne rigate**

**¼ lb (110 g) bacon, cut into narrow strips**

**½ cup (125 mL) frozen peas, thawed**

**5 oz (150 g) uncooked peeled shrimp, cut in half if large**

**1½ tbsp (20 mL) butter**

**½ cup (125 mL) ricotta cheese**

**salt and freshly ground black pepper**

**1 tbsp (15 mL) grated Parmesan cheese**

**1** Cook penne in boiling salted water.
**2** In a large frying pan sauté bacon until the fat melts. Add thawed peas and sauté for 1 to 2 minutes before stirring in shrimp. Cook, stirring, until just done. Add butter and lower the heat so that butter melts slowly.
**3** In a bowl combine ricotta, salt, pepper and Parmesan. Just before serving, add 2 or 3 tbsp (30–45 mL) boiling pasta water and whisk in. Drain penne when *al dente* and toss it with the ricotta. Then add bacon, shrimp and peas and toss once more before serving.

**SERVES 4**

# LASAGNETTE WITH MUSHROOMS AND CHICKEN

**¼ cup (60 mL) milk**

**½ tsp (2.5 mL) dried tarragon or 2 tsp (10 mL) chopped fresh**

**1 lb (450 g) lasagnette**

**2 tbsp (30 mL) butter**

**2 cloves garlic**

**½ lb (225 g) chicken fillet or breast, sliced**

**1¼ cups (310 mL) button mushrooms, sliced**

**1½ tsp (7 mL) porcini mushrooms, soaked in hot water to cover for 30 minutes, then chopped (optional)**

**salt, pepper and nutmeg**

**2 cups (500 mL) cream**

**few sprigs fresh tarragon, for garnish**

**1** Put milk and tarragon in a small saucepan and bring to the boil. Remove from heat and let steep.
**2** Begin cooking lasagnette in boiling salted water.
**3** In a frying pan melt butter and gently sauté garlic, chicken and mushrooms until chicken is golden and cooked through. Discard garlic cloves and add chopped porcini mushrooms and the strained soaking liquid. Add salt, pepper and nutmeg to taste and stir for 10 seconds or so before pouring in cream and tarragon milk. Stir well, bring to the boil and simmer until sauce thickens.
**4** Drain pasta when it is *al dente* and transfer to a warm serving plate. Taste sauce for seasonings, then add to pasta and toss. Serve decorated with tarragon.

**SERVES 4**

≈ **PENNE WITH SHRIMP AND BACON**

*This combination appears to break all the rules – bacon with shellfish, cheese with seafood and hot with cold – but with delicious results. Cooking time is minimal and here is one instance where frozen peas are preferable to fresh, as their texture when thawed allows for a good saturation by the bacon fat.*

*Lasagnette with Mushrooms and Chicken*

# SAUCES

The secret's in the sauce, and there's no denying that it's hard to beat a delicious bowl of pasta served with your favorite sauce. The variety available means that there is always a sauce that is right for the occasion. Some sauces are traditionally served as part of particular dishes, so we have included whole dishes here, as well as individual sauces.

## PESTO GENOVESE

*Pesto is traditionally served with trenette, but can go on any ribbon pasta and is very good on cheese-filled ravioli. It can be used in soups, on salads and steamed vegetables, and is perfect for drizzling over baked tomatoes. It is essential to use fresh young basil, and the sauce is at its best when a quality extra virgin olive oil is used. For variations, try pepato cheese instead of plain pecorino to give a more piquant flavor, or substitute tender spinach leaves for some of the basil.*

**pinch salt (optional)**
**1 bunch fresh basil leaves, roughly chopped**
**2 cloves garlic**
**⅓ cup (85 mL) olive oil**
**¼ cup (60 mL) pine nuts, lightly toasted**
**½ cup (125 mL) freshly grated Parmesan cheese**
**½ cup (125 mL) freshly grated pecorino cheese**
**½ tsp (2.5 mL) toasted bread crumbs
(if using food processor method)**

**1 USING A PESTLE AND MORTAR:** Add a pinch of salt to the basil, garlic, 1 tbsp (15 mL) oil and a few pine nuts and begin crushing. Continue adding pine nuts and oil until you have a smooth texture. Blend in cheeses and stir well.

**2 USING A FOOD PROCESSOR OR BLENDER:** Add basil, garlic, bread crumbs, pine nuts and cheeses. Chop thoroughly, and continue to blend as you gradually pour in olive oil. Continue until a mayonnaise-like texture is obtained.

**SERVES 4**

**≈ PESTO**

*Pesto can be kept successfully for 5 to 7 days in the refrigerator if the surface is covered with a thin layer of olive oil, and it can be frozen if you omit the cheeses and stir them in after defrosting. However, aficionados maintain that it should be made just before needed, and that storing the sauce changes the composition of the ingredients.*

*Ingredients for Pesto Genovese*

*Sauce of Four Cheeses*

# SAUCE OF FOUR CHEESES

**1½ tbsp (20 mL) butter**

**1 tsp (5 mL) all-purpose flour**

**¾ cup (185 mL) milk**

**¾ cup (185 mL) shredded fontina cheese**

**¾ cup (185 mL) shredded provolone cheese**

**¾ cup (185 mL) shredded Emmenthaler cheese**

**¾ cup (185 mL) shredded mozzarella cheese**

**freshly grated Parmesan cheese, to serve**

**1** Heat butter in a saucepan and when it starts to foam, stir in flour. Cook for half a minute and then stir in milk. Continue cooking over gentle heat, stirring, until thickened and smooth. Remove from heat and beat in all the cheeses except Parmesan.
**2** Place the saucepan over a pot of boiling water and heat until sauce is smooth, stirring often. Don't boil once the cheeses have been added or the sauce will separate. Serve over hot pasta with the Parmesan.

**SERVES 4 ENTRÉES**

# SORREL AND SPINACH SAUCE

**½ lb (225 g) fresh sorrel, leaves only**

**½ lb (225 g) fresh spinach, leaves only**

**salt**

**3 tbsp (45 mL) butter**

**3 tbsp (45 mL) olive oil**

**1 tbsp (15 mL) finely chopped fresh parsley**

**1 tbsp (15 mL) finely chopped fresh basil**

**freshly ground black pepper**

**pinch ground nutmeg**

**⅓ cup (85 mL) cream**

1  Rinse sorrel and spinach under cold water and shake off excess water. Put in a large pot with a pinch of salt but no extra water and cook gently, covered, until limp and tender. Drain and chop finely.

2  Melt butter and oil in a large frying pan and add sorrel, spinach and herbs. Season with a little salt, lots of black pepper and a good pinch of nutmeg. Cook gently for 5 minutes, then add cream and simmer for 5 minutes more.

**SERVES 4 TO 6**

# CHEESE AND NUT SAUCE

*This is a good coating sauce. It can be made in advance, but its success depends on using fresh walnuts (preferably just from the shell) and fresh basil. It can be served on vegetables, too, and is particularly fine on green beans.*

½ cup (125 mL) shelled walnuts

¼ cup (60 mL) pine nuts, roasted

1 tsp (5 mL) toasted fresh bread crumbs

3 tbsp (45 mL) fresh basil leaves

salt and freshly ground black pepper

1 clove garlic, crushed

3 tbsp (45 mL) olive oil

1 tbsp (15 mL) freshly grated Parmesan cheese

¼ cup (60 mL) ricotta cheese

1  In a food processor or blender, place nuts, bread crumbs, basil, salt and pepper. Blend until they form a coarse paste. Add garlic and oil, and mix well.

2  Transfer to a bowl and stir in Parmesan and ricotta. Continue to mix until the sauce is smooth. Taste for salt and pepper, and add a little more Parmesan if a sharper flavor is preferred.

3  Serve over any hot pasta, adding 1 tbsp (15 mL) of the pasta's cooking water to heat and thin (so it will coat the pasta).

**SERVES 4 ENTRÉES**

# PICCHI-PACCHI

⅓ cup (85 mL) olive oil

1 large onion, thinly sliced

1 clove garlic, crushed

4 anchovy fillets, drained and soaked in milk for 45 minutes

1⅔ cups (415 mL) canned Italian peeled tomatoes, drained and chopped

1 sprig fresh basil

salt and freshly ground black pepper

1  In a large pan heat oil and sauté onion and garlic until soft.

2  Add drained anchovies and cook for 1 to 2 minutes, breaking them up with the spoon as you stir.

3  Add tomatoes and basil, season lightly and simmer, covered, for 20 minutes or so, until smooth and thick. Adjust seasoning. No grated cheese is served with this sauce.

**SERVES 4**

# BAKED TOMATO SAUCE

3⅓ cups (835 mL) canned Italian peeled tomatoes, drained and mashed

2 cloves garlic, crushed

1 onion, finely chopped

2 tsp (10 mL) finely chopped fresh basil or 1 tsp (5 mL) dried

¼ cup (60 mL) olive oil

chili flakes

⅓ cup (85 mL) fresh bread crumbs mixed with ⅓ cup (85 mL) grated Parmesan cheese

1  Preheat oven to 400°F (200°C).

2  Put tomatoes, garlic, onion, basil and oil in an ovenproof dish and sprinkle with a few chili flakes. Stir to combine. Sprinkle bread crumb mixture over the top and bake, uncovered, for 30 minutes.

3  Don't break up the crust until the sauce is being tossed through the pasta; large crunchy bits should remain.

**SERVES 4**

≈ **PICCHI-PACCHI**

*Picchi-pacchi is a rich, full-flavored sauce that can be served on most types of pasta, but coming from Sicily it more often than not appears on spaghetti. There is a version that includes fried eggplant, and another has black olives thrown in for the last 5 minutes of cooking.*

≈ **BAKED TOMATO SAUCE**

*This sauce has a unique flavor that stove-top tomato sauces can't match. It can be easily adapted by adding olives, salami, sautéed vegetables, shrimp or just about anything, and it complements all types of pasta.*

≈ **RED PESTO**

*Red Pesto is a good
coating sauce with an
intriguing tang to it.
Served over pasta shapes
or ribbons, it makes a
piquant first course well
suited to precede a main
meal of broiled or baked
tuna steaks. It keeps well
in the refrigerator for up
to 4 days.*

# SAUCE OF LEEKS, GRUYÈRE AND CREAM

**1½ tbsp (20 mL) unsalted butter**

**1 clove garlic**

**white part of 1 large leek, thinly sliced**

**3 tbsp (45 mL) all-purpose flour**

**salt, white pepper and nutmeg**

**¾ cup (185 mL) milk**

**2 cups (500 mL) cream**

**1 cup (250 mL) grated Gruyère cheese**

**1** Melt butter in a saucepan and add garlic and leek. Over low heat gently cook leek, stirring often, until golden and softened, about 8 minutes.

**2** Stir in the flour and season to taste with salt, pepper and nutmeg. Cook until flour changes color slightly.

**3** Remove garlic clove and then gradually add the milk, stirring all the time. When sauce is smooth and thick, pour in cream. Bring to the boil, lower the heat and cook for 5 minutes.

**4** Add Gruyère and cook, stirring, until cheese has melted. Remove from heat and cool slightly before serving. This sauce keeps well refrigerated for up to 4 days.

**SERVES 4**

# RED PESTO

**½ oz (14 g) anchovy fillets, soaked in milk for 45 minutes**

**large pinch salt**

**1 clove garlic, crushed**

**⅓ cup (85 mL) pine nuts, toasted**

**1½ heaping tbsp (25 mL) dried bread crumbs**

**6½ oz (180 g) drained red pimiento (canned or bottled), roughly chopped**

**⅔ cup (165 mL) chopped tomatoes, drained and seeded**

**2 tsp (10 mL) capers**

**1 tsp (5 mL) dried oregano**

**1 tbsp (15 mL) chopped fresh parsley**

**3–4 tbsp (45–60 mL) red wine vinegar**

**½ cup (125 mL) olive oil**

**1** In a blender or food processor blend drained anchovies, salt, garlic, pine nuts and bread crumbs. Add pimiento and tomatoes and process until a red paste forms.

**2** Add capers, oregano and parsley and blend. Add vinegar. Gradually add oil and mix until sauce is the consistency of pesto.

**3** Stir into hot pasta, adding 1 tsp (5 mL) of the pasta's cooking water first, to make coating easier.

**SERVES 4**

# SPAGHETTI ALLA PUTTANESCA

**⅓ cup (85 mL) olive oil**

**2 cloves garlic, crushed**

**pinch chili flakes**

**6 anchovy fillets, drained and soaked in milk for 30 minutes**

**1⅔ cups (415 mL) canned Italian peeled tomatoes**

**⅔ cup (165 mL) black olives, sliced**

**1 tbsp (15 mL) capers**

**1 sprig fresh oregano or ¼ tsp (1 mL) dried**

**1 lb (450 g) fresh spaghetti or ⅔ lb (300 g) dried**

**2 tsp (10 mL) chopped fresh parsley**

**1** Heat oil in a large frying pan and gently sauté garlic and chili. Drain anchovies of excess milk and add to the pan, mashing them as you stir.

**2** Take the tomatoes out of the can one by one, squeezing them over the sink to remove seeds and some of the juice, before adding to the pan. Save remaining juice in the can to moisten the sauce as it is cooking. Add olives, capers and oregano and cook over medium heat for 10 minutes.

**3** Cook spaghetti in boiling salted water until *al dente*. Drain and transfer to a warm serving dish. Pour sauce over the top, toss and add parsley.

**SERVES 4**

## MARINARA SAUCE

*A marinara sauce is basically tomatoes and garlic reduced to a rich sauce. You can have an artichoke marinara, one made with olives or, of course, a seafood marinara.*

**¼ cup (60 mL) olive oil**

**2 cloves garlic, crushed**

**1 small onion, chopped**

**¼ cup (60 mL) chopped fresh parsley, or half parsley and half fresh basil**

**6 large tomatoes, peeled, seeded and chopped, or 3⅓ cups (835 mL) canned Italian peeled tomatoes, drained and pulped**

**pinch sugar**

**salt and freshly ground black pepper**

**1** In a large saucepan heat oil and sauté garlic and onion until soft and golden, about 10 minutes; do not brown.

**2** Add herbs, tomatoes, sugar, salt and pepper. Simmer, stirring occasionally, until sauce is thick and mellow, about 30 minutes.

**SERVES 4**

## PISTACHIO MAYONNAISE

**3 egg yolks**

**1 cup (250 mL) extra virgin olive oil**

**salt and freshly ground black pepper**

**juice of ½ lemon**

**1 tbsp (15 mL) finely chopped fresh basil**

**3 tbsp (45 mL) finely chopped fresh parsley**

**3 tbsp (45 mL) ground pistachio nuts**

**1** Whisk egg yolks in a bowl. Continue to whisk and pour in oil in a very slow trickle, until it has all been absorbed. Still whisking, add salt, pepper and lemon juice to taste. Add basil, parsley and nuts and stir until sauce is smooth and very thick.

**2** If the mayonnaise looks like it's about to curdle, finish making it anyway. Then beat another egg yolk in a clean bowl and gradually whisk in the curdled sauce. The mayonnaise will keep, covered and chilled, for up to 24 hours.

**SERVES 4 TO 6**

*Pistachio Mayonnaise*

**≈ PISTACHIO MAYONNAISE**

*This is delicious served over hot fresh herb fettuccine or with cold shellfish and fresh peas in a pasta salad. It is less successful if made with a food processor or blender. Perhaps it's the moisture in the fresh herbs being crushed that disrupts the balance of things; whatever the reason, the sauce is more likely to curdle if made with a machine, and the texture and color also suffer.*

**≈ REHEATING PASTA**

*A useful way to reheat cold pasta is to put it directly into a saucepan or frying pan with the sauce and stir just enough for it all to heat through well.*

# BUCATINI ALL'AMATRICIANA

*This sauce from the town of Amatrice depends on a light tomato flavor and the crispness of the bacon. It used to be made with not much chili at all, but as tastes changed, a hotter sauce has gradually evolved. For variation add 2 or 3 tbsp (30–45 mL) chopped parsley or some garlic, both of which nicely complement the basic ingredients.*

**1 lb (450 g) bucatini**

**2 tbsp (30 mL) olive oil**

**1 small onion, finely chopped**

**1 piece hot chili, or chili flakes to taste**

**2½ cups (625 mL) canned Italian peeled tomatoes, drained and chopped**

**¼ lb (110 g) thickly sliced pancetta or bacon, diced**

**3 tbsp (45 mL) freshly grated Parmesan cheese**

**1**  Begin cooking bucatini in boiling water.

**2**  Heat half the oil in a frying pan and sauté onion and chili until softened. Add tomatoes and simmer for about 7 minutes; they shouldn't be stewed into a rich sauce for this recipe.

**3**  Meanwhile, fry pancetta in the remaining oil until crisp. Keep warm.

**4**  When the pasta is *al dente*, drain and place in a warm bowl. Stir in Parmesan, sauce and lastly pancetta.

**SERVES 4**

**≈ FETTUCCINE WITH PEAS AND HAM IN AN EGG SAUCE**

*This is also good with some sliced button mushrooms fried with the leeks.*

# FETTUCCINE WITH PEAS AND HAM IN EGG SAUCE

**2 cups (500 mL) fresh or frozen young peas**

**1 cup (250 mL) chicken stock**

**¼ lb (110 g) unsalted butter**

**2 leeks, white part only, thinly sliced**

**¼ lb (110 g) sliced ham, julienned**

**1 lb (450 g) fresh fettuccine or ¾ lb (340 g) dried**

**2 medium eggs**

**¾ cup (185 mL) freshly grated Parmesan cheese**

**salt and freshly ground black pepper**

**1**  Cook peas in chicken stock until tender. Set aside with 3 tbsp (45 mL) cooking liquid.

**2**  Melt butter and gently fry leeks until soft and golden. Stir in peas, stock and ham. Cover and keep warm.

**3**  Begin cooking fettuccine in boiling salted water. While it is cooking, beat eggs with half the Parmesan and season with salt and pepper. Place in a large serving dish and keep warm.

**4**  When the pasta is just cooked, drain it (not too well; some water can remain) and toss immediately with egg mixture. Quickly stir in ham and pea sauce. Serve with remaining Parmesan and extra pepper.

**SERVES 4 AS A LIGHT MEAL**

# SPAGHETTINI WITH LEMON, HAM AND CREAM

**⅔ lb (300 g) dried spaghettini or 1 lb (450 g) fresh**

**⅓ cup (85 mL) unsalted butter**

**5 oz (150 g) sliced strong ham, cut into thin strips**

**1 cup (250 mL) cream**

**1 tbsp (15 mL) finely chopped fresh parsley**

**grated rind of 1 lemon**

**salt and freshly ground black pepper**

**3 tbsp (45 mL) grated Parmesan cheese**

**1**  Begin cooking spaghettini in boiling salted water.

**2**  Melt butter in a large deep frying pan and add ham. Cook for 30 seconds before adding the cream, parsley and lemon rind. Season with salt and pepper and cook for 1 to 2 minutes more, until thick and smooth.

**3**  When pasta is *al dente*, drain and add it to the pan with Parmesan. Toss quickly to coat well and heat through. Serve with additional grated Parmesan.

**SERVES 4**

*Bucatini All'Amatriciana*

*Paglia e Fieno with Bacon, Peas and Mushrooms*

# PAGLIA E FIENO WITH BACON, PEAS AND MUSHROOMS

½ lb (225 g) fresh plain fettuccine or
⅓ lb (150 g) dried

½ lb (225 g) fresh spinach fettuccine or
⅓ lb (150 g) dried

1¼ cups (310 mL) shelled peas, fresh or
frozen

½ lb (225 g) bacon, cut into strips

1½ tsp (7 mL) dried porcini mushrooms,
soaked in

3 tbsp (45 mL) warm water (optional)

2½ cups (625 mL) button mushrooms, sliced

1 clove garlic, crushed

1 tsp (5 mL) freshly ground black pepper

1 bunch fresh parsley, finely chopped

2¼ cups (560 mL) cream

grated Parmesan, to serve

**1** Cook peas until tender in a large
saucepan of boiling salted water; remove
with a slotted spoon and set aside, reserving
cooking liquid.

**2** Fry bacon gently until crisp.

**3** Squeeze soaked dried porcini over the
pot, chop them finely and add to the pot with
remaining soaking juice and fresh mushrooms.
Stir in garlic and pepper and cook briefly. Toss
in parsley and cook for 30 seconds.

**4** Add cream and cook, stirring, until the
sauce comes to the boil. Boil until
thickened and reduced, 5 to 8 minutes.

**5** Begin cooking fettuccine in the water
used for the peas. When *al dente*, drain and
transfer to a warm serving dish. Add the
sauce and stir. Serve with freshly grated
Parmesan.

**SERVES 4**

# PENNE ALL'ARRABBIATA

**1 tbsp (15 mL) dried porcini mushrooms
(optional)**

**3 tbsp (45 mL) olive oil**

**1 onion, finely chopped**

**2 cloves garlic, crushed**

**¼ lb (110 g) pancetta or unsmoked bacon,
cut into strips**

**2½ cups (625 mL) canned Italian peeled
tomatoes, drained and chopped**

**¼ tsp (1 mL) chili flakes**

**1 lb (450 g) penne**

**⅓ cup (85 mL) grated pecorino cheese**

**3 tbsp (45 mL) butter, cut into slivers and
kept cold**

**1** If using porcini, soak in 1 tbsp (15 mL)
water for 1 hour and then cut into thin
strips. (Reserve the juice for another use.)

**2** Heat oil in a large saucepan and sauté
onion and garlic gently for 5 minutes. Add
pancetta and sauté for 5 minutes more.

**3** Add porcini, tomatoes and chili flakes
and simmer over moderate heat until
thickened and rich, 20 to 30 minutes. Taste
for seasoning and add more chili if you like.
If the sauce appears to be drying out, stir in
1½ – 2½ tbsp (20 – 45 mL) pasta cooking
water.

**4** Cook pasta in boiling salted water.
Remove from heat and drain when it is just
*al dente*.

**5** When ready to serve, toss penne and
pecorino with sauce and stir. Stir in butter
and serve.

**SERVES 4**

## ≈ COMBINING SAUCE AND PASTA

*A step practiced by a lot of Italian cooks is to unite the
sauce with the pasta immediately after cooking. This keeps
everything hot and results in a quick and even
distribution of flavors; you can save a little of the sauce
for decoration, if desired. When using a cold sauce with
hot pasta, for example pesto, quickly mix a couple of
spoonsful of cooking water into the sauce to help it coat
more readily.*

# SAUCE FROM BOLOGNA

**¼ cup (60 mL) butter**

**1 small onion, finely chopped**

**1 stalk celery, finely chopped**

**1 small carrot, finely chopped**

**2 oz (60 g) pancetta or bacon,
finely chopped**

**1 bay leaf**

**10 oz (300 g) lean ground beef**

**1½ tsp (7.5 mL) all-purpose flour**

**½ cup (125 mL) dry red wine**

**1 tbsp (15 mL) dried porcini mushrooms,
soaked in a little warm water for 1 hour,
then chopped (optional)**

**salt and freshly ground black pepper**

**pinch nutmeg or cloves**

**½ cup (125 mL) beef stock or consommé**

**½ cup (125 mL) milk**

**3 tbsp (45 mL) cream**

**1 chicken liver, finely chopped**

**1** In a large pot melt butter and gently
sauté onion, celery, carrot, pancetta and bay
leaf for 8 to 10 minutes.

**2** Add ground beef, increase the heat
slightly and cook until golden brown.
Sprinkle in flour, stir and cook for 30
seconds before adding wine. Stir over high
heat until most of the liquid is reduced.

**3** Add porcini plus the soaking liquid and
taste for salt before seasoning. Add nutmeg
and half the stock and simmer over low
heat, covered, for 1½ hours.

**4** Stir from time to time and add
remaining stock as you go. Add milk after
1 hour and adjust seasonings. Just before
serving stir in cream and chicken liver and
cook, uncovered, for a final minute or two.

**SERVES 4**

## ≈ SAUCE FROM BOLOGNA

*The true Bolognese sauce
bears little resemblance to
that found outside Italy;
it's not even served with
spaghetti, but tagliatelle,
again the creation of
Bologna. Like the city,
the sauce is mellow and
sophisticated. Its flavor
comes from long gentle
cooking, and the addition
of milk softens and
sweetens it. No garlic is
necessary and tomatoes
aren't used, although
some cooks like to add a
spoonful or two of tomato
paste for extra richness
and color.*

## ≈ SAUCE CONSISTENCY

*Pasta sauces should have
a good thick coating
consistency, so where
possible use 18% or
whipping cream (35%).
Most recipes just say
"cream" and will work
with 10% cream, but
cooking time is longer.
When using 18% or
whipping cream, reduce
cooking time slightly.*

# FINE FARE

A deliciously filling meal can be made with pasta of all descriptions.
Serve long pasta (fettuccine, taglierini, spaghetti or linguine) with a good
coating sauce based on oil, tomato, cream or soft melting cheeses. Twisted
or hollow pasta (fusilli, zitoni or rotelli) is best with chunky sauces. Long
fine strands (vermicelli or angel's hair) are delicious with clinging sauces
made of butter and cheese, raw tomato or an egg base, and wide flat
noodles, like pappardelle or lasagnatte, go with gutsy meaty sauces.

## ≈ COOKING FOR MANY

*If you are cooking for a
crowd, precook pasta in
batches, then oil it lightly
and keep it warm in the
oven covered with a damp
cloth.*

## FARFALLE WITH SMOKED SALMON AND MASCARPONE

**⅔ lb (300 g) farfalle**

**2 leeks, white part only, thinly sliced**

**3 tbsp (45 mL) butter**

**½ red pepper, julienned**

**1⅔ cups (415 mL) mascarpone
or whipping cream**

**½ lb (225 g) smoked salmon,
cut into thin strips**

**salt and white pepper**

**chopped fennel tops (optional)**

**1** Cook farfalle in boiling salted water until
*al dente.*

**2** Cook leeks gently in melted butter for
a few minutes, being careful not to brown
them. Reserve a few pieces of the red pepper
for decoration, and add the rest to the leeks.
Cook for 30 seconds more.

**3** Add mascarpone and bring to the boil.
Stir in most of the smoked salmon (keep
a few slices to decorate) and cook just long
enough to heat through. Taste for salt and
add if needed. Add a pinch of pepper. Toss
in the fennel tops.

**4** Add to the drained pasta and decorate
with reserved pepper and salmon.

**SERVES 4**

*Pasta and Bean Soup*

# PASTA AND BEAN SOUP

*Pasta and beans are common to many regions where they each have their special recipes. In Venice they like their pasta and beans flavored with a touch of cinnamon and the bone from a Parma ham, a subtle but unforgettable flavor sometimes enhanced with Parmesan cheese.*

**½ lb (225 g) borlotti beans, soaked in water overnight**

**1 prosciutto or ham bone**

**1 onion, chopped**

**pinch cinnamon**

**cayenne pepper**

**2 tsp (10 mL) olive oil**

**2 cups (500 mL) chicken stock**

**¼ lb (110 g) tagliatelle, plain or spinach, broken into 1¼ – 1½ inch (3 – 4 cm) lengths**

**1** Drain and rinse beans, cover with cold water in a saucepan and bring to the boil. Stir, then boil for 15 minutes.

**2** Drain beans and transfer to a large pot with ham bone, onion, cinnamon, pinch of cayenne, olive oil and stock. Add cold water to cover. Cover pot well and simmer until beans are cooked and have begun to thicken the stock. Remove bone and cut off any meat from it. Flake this and return to the pot; discard bone.

**3** Taste for seasonings; salt may be needed, depending on the bone used. Bring the soup back to the boil, then toss in pasta and cook until it is *al dente*. Remove pot from heat and let stand for 1 to 2 minutes before serving.

**SERVES 5 TO 6**

# BAKED MUSHROOM AND RICOTTA PARCELS

## PASTA

1⅔ cups (415 mL) all-purpose flour

salt

2 eggs plus 2 yolks, beaten together

1½ tbsp (20 mL) butter, melted

1¼ cups (310 mL) milk

extra melted butter

## FILLING

3 tbsp (45 mL) butter

1 lb (450 g) button mushrooms, sliced

¼ tsp (1 mL) each salt, freshly ground black pepper and nutmeg

3 tbsp (45 mL) toasted fresh bread crumbs

¼ cup (60 mL) finely chopped fresh parsley

1½ cups (375 mL) ricotta cheese

½ cup (125 mL) mascarpone

1 tbsp (15 mL) grated Parmesan cheese

1 egg plus 1 yolk, beaten together

## TOPPING

½ cup (125 mL) grated Parmesan cheese

¼ cup plus 1 tbsp (75 mL) butter, melted

**1  To Prepare Pasta:** Sift flour and a pinch of salt into a bowl. Add beaten eggs and butter and stir to combine. Gradually mix in milk until a thick batter is obtained. Continue to beat 7 to 8 minutes more to get a smooth consistency. Let batter stand for at least 5 minutes.

**2**  Heat some of the extra butter in a small frying pan, then pour in enough batter to thinly cover the bottom. Gently cook on both sides, pancake fashion, until golden. Remove from the pan and repeat with remaining batter, buttering as you go. There should be 6 to 8 cooked sheets, depending on the size of your pan. Trim each one neatly into a square and set aside.

**1  To Prepare Filling:** Heat butter in a frying pan and fry mushrooms until golden but still crisp. Season with salt, pepper and

nutmeg and stir in bread crumbs and parsley. Transfer the mixture to a bowl and mix with ricotta, mascarpone, Parmesan and eggs. Combine well.

**4**  Preheat oven to 400°F (200°C).

**5**  Place equal amount of filling in the center of each fried pasta sheet, then fold the corners into the middle, like an envelope, to form a parcel. Arrange the parcels side by side in a buttered shallow ovenproof dish. Sprinkle the tops with Parmesan and melted butter and bake until golden, about 15 minutes.

**SERVES 4**

# CHICKEN, LEEK AND CHICKPEA SOUP

4 cups (1 L) chicken stock

¼ lb (110 g) tiny pasta shapes (ditalini, tiny shells)

1½ tbsp (20 mL) butter

1 leek, white part only, sliced

1 clove garlic

½ cup (125 mL) roasted chickpeas

1 tbsp (15 mL) all-purpose flour

3 heaping tbsp (50 mL) finely chopped fresh Italian parsley

salt and freshly ground black pepper

pinch cayenne pepper

½ lb (225 g) chopped cooked chicken meat

**1**  Put chicken stock in a saucepan and bring to the boil. Add pasta and cook until barely done. Remove with a slotted spoon. Leave stock simmering.

**2**  Meanwhile, melt butter in a large saucepan and gently sauté leek and garlic until golden, not brown. Add chickpeas, toss for a minute and then sprinkle with the flour. Fry for 10 seconds or so, then gradually blend in boiling stock.

**3**  Add parsley, salt and cayenne and a good half dozen grinds of the pepper mill. Add pasta and chicken meat and bring back to the boil before serving.

**SERVES 4**

≈ **HEALTHY BAKED PARCELS**

*This method of baking filled pasta parcels is great for the diet-conscious, as it does away with the need for the coating sauce that conventional cannelloni require. Just be careful not to over-bake, as this will make your pasta dry and tough. Make sure you don't use too much butter when cooking the sheets.*

≈ **CHICKEN, LEEK AND CHICKPEA SOUP**

*To roast chickpeas, toss drained canned chickpeas in a lightly oiled frying pan until golden. The subtle flavor of this soup can be made even more interesting by using fresh coriander instead of parsley, and frying a pinch of chili with the leek.*

# SPICY RICOTTA AGNOLOTTI IN HERB LEAF PASTA

### PASTA

2½ cups (625 mL) all-purpose flour

pinch salt

3 eggs, lightly beaten

nicely shaped leaves of any flat-leaved herb (Italian parsley, chervil or coriander), reserve some for decoration

1 egg, beaten

### FILLING

2 cups (500 mL) ricotta

3 tbsp (45 mL) grated Parmesan cheese

pinch grated nutmeg

pinch chili powder

salt

approximately ½ cup (125 mL) fresh bread crumbs

### TO FINISH

½ cup (125 mL) light olive oil

4 cloves garlic

freshly grated Parmesan cheese

fresh herbs

**1 TO PREPARE PASTA:** Mix flour and salt in a food processor for a second or two. Add whole eggs and continue to process until a smooth ball forms. Incorporate more flour or a little water, if necessary. Cover dough with a damp cloth or plastic wrap and let stand for 30 minutes.

**2** Divide dough into four pieces. Working with one piece at a time, roll out until the dough is twice as thick as you want your pasta to be. You can use a long rolling pin, but a more consistent result is obtained with a hand-cranked pasta machine. Do not flour the surface before the next step.

**3** Take some herb leaves and discard thick or fleshy stems, then separate into attractive sections of about ½ inch (1 cm) each. Place at 1¼–1½ inch (3–4 cm) intervals over half the pasta sheet. Fold the plain half over the leaves and roll out. It may be necessary to roll the pasta several times to press the

herb leaves, which will take on a delicate stretched appearance.

**4** Cover each sheet of pasta with a tea-towel.

**5** Using a pastry cutter of 3¼–4 inch (8–10 cm) diameter, cut out circles over the herbs on the pasta sheets. As you work, set aside and cover the finished circles.

**6 TO PREPARE FILLING:** Mix first five ingredients together, then add bread crumbs until a light but manageable texture is reached.

**7** Lay out half a dozen circles, paint their edges with egg and place some filling across the center. Fold each one over to encase filling, press edges together and trim with a zig-zag pastry wheel. Set aside, uncovered, until all the agnolotti are finished.

**8 TO FINISH:** Heat oil in a large pan or wok and gently sauté garlic over low heat. Discard garlic and keep oil warm.

**9** Cook agnolotti in boiling salted water until *al dente*. Drain, then transfer to the pan with the olive oil and toss to coat.

**10** Serve immediately with a sprinkling of herb leaves and Parmesan.

**SERVES 4**

# TAGLIATELLE WITH ZUCCHINI AND BASIL

1⅓ lbs (600 g) small zucchini, cut into
1½ x ½ inch (4 x 1 cm) sticks

¼ cup plus 1 tbsp (75 mL) unsalted butter

½ cup (125 mL) vegetable oil

1 tbsp (15 mL) all-purpose flour

1 cup (250 mL) milk

1 lb (450 g) fresh tagliatelle or ⅔ lb (300 g) dried

½ cup (125 mL) cream

½ cup (125 mL) fresh basil, finely chopped

**1** Put zucchini sticks in a colander, sprinkle with a little salt and leave to drain for 30 minutes; pat dry with cloth.

**2** Heat a little of the butter and oil in a large pan and fry zucchini until brown but still crisp. Remove from heat and set aside.

**3** Melt rest of oil and butter in a saucepan. Add flour and cook, stirring, until the paste is smooth and slightly colored. Gradually add milk, stirring to break up any lumps. Cook until thickened and smooth.

**4** Begin cooking tagliatelle in boiling salted water. Add cream to the white sauce and bring to the boil. When thickened, remove from heat and stir in zucchini and basil. When the pasta is *al dente*, drain and transfer to a warm serving dish. Pour the sauce over it and serve immediately.

**SERVES 4**

≈ **TAGLIATELLE WITH ZUCCHINI AND BASIL**

*This has a delicate balance of flavors that should not be missed when young basil is available. It is an excellent dish to precede a main course of lamb's kidneys or liver.*

*Tagliatelle with Zucchini and Basil*

*Carrot-flavored pasta has a fresh, slightly nutty flavor and can be served a number of different ways. Here, with a cream sauce, it is rich and sweet.*

*Fresh Carrot Pasta*

# FRESH CARROT PASTA WITH CREAM AND MINT

## PASTA

½ lb (225 g) carrots, peeled and diced

2 eggs

2 tsp (10 mL) vegetable oil

1½ cups (375 mL) semolina

1½ cups (375 mL) all-purpose flour

1 tsp (5 mL) salt

pinch nutmeg

pinch white pepper

## SAUCE

½ lb (225 g) carrots, peeled and julienned

3 tbsp (45 mL) butter

1 tbsp (15 mL) finely chopped fresh mint

1¼ cups (310 mL) cream

salt and white pepper

**1 TO PREPARE PASTA:** Purée carrots finely in a food processor, add the rest of the ingredients and process to form a dough.

**2** To mix by hand, place flours and seasonings in a pile on a work surface and make a well in the center. Add eggs, oil and carrot purée and begin working into the dry ingredients with a fork until a roughly formed dough results. Now take the dough and begin kneading by hand, incorporating extra flour if needed, to form a smooth, elastic ball. This will take 8 to 10 minutes. Cover with a damp cloth or plastic wrap and let stand for 30 minutes.

**3** Divide the dough into three pieces. Working with one piece at a time, roll out to very thin sheets using a rolling pin or a hand-cranked pasta machine. Trim to rectangles approximately 8 inches (20 cm) long; then cover and let stand for 15 minutes.

**4** If cutting by hand, roll up each rectangle along its length and slice off sections about ¼ inch (0.5 cm) in width. These will unroll to become taglierini. If using a pasta machine, cut to desired width. Dust the ribbons lightly with flour and let stand, uncovered, to dry slightly.

**5 TO PREPARE SAUCE:** Blanch carrots in boiling water until tender-crisp. In a saucepan melt butter and gently sauté mint for 30 seconds. Add cream and simmer, uncovered, to thicken. Season the sauce lightly and add the carrots. Put pasta on to cook in boiling salted water. Drain pasta when it is *al dente*, stir in a little vegetable oil and then transfer to warm plates. Pour on the sauce and serve at once.

**SERVES 5 TO 6**

# SEAFOOD PASTA SALAD

⅓ lb (150 g) fresh fettuccine or ¼ lb (110 g) dried (include some tomato flavored if possible), broken into short lengths

5 oz (150 g) squid, cleaned and cut into rings

5 oz (150 g) baby clams, bottled or canned, drained

¾ cup (185 mL) milk

1 tbsp (15 mL) olive oil

½ lb (225 g) cooked shrimp, cut in half if large

1 very small red onion, thinly sliced

1 small red pepper, sliced

1 stalk celery, sliced

1½–2½ tbsp (20–40 mL) chopped fresh dill

1½ cups (375 mL) cherry tomatoes, yellow or red

### DRESSING

¾ cup (185 mL) olive oil

2 cloves garlic, crushed

juice of 1 lemon

3 tbsp (45 mL) white wine vinegar

salt and freshly ground black pepper

**1** Cook pasta in boiling salted water until *al dente*. Drain, rinse under cold water and drain again. Transfer to a large serving bowl and stir in a little of the olive oil.

**2** Soak squid rings and clams in milk for at least 30 minutes, drain, and then fry them gently in 1 tbsp (15 mL) olive oil until the squid is opaque and tender. Transfer to the salad bowl.

**3** Add shrimp, onion, pepper and celery and toss lightly.

**4** TO PREPARE DRESSING: In a screw-top jar combine dressing ingredients and shake well. Pour over salad. Add half the dill and toss lightly but thoroughly to coat the ingredients. Chill for 1 hour or more. When ready to serve, decorate with remaining dill and tomatoes.

**SERVES 3 TO 4**

# PASTA SALAD WITH CHICKEN, SHRIMP AND MELON

¼ lb (110 g) elbow macaroni or other medium-size pasta shape

vegetable oil

10 oz (300 g) chicken fillets

salt and freshly ground black pepper

2 tbsp (30 mL) butter

1 honeydew melon

10 oz (300 g) small cooked shrimp, peeled and deveined

1 cup (250 mL) finely sliced celery

### DRESSING

3 tbsp (45 mL) mayonnaise

¼ cup (60 mL) plain yogurt

2 tbsp (30 mL) cream

¼ tsp (1 mL) chili sauce, or to taste

1 tsp (5 mL) chopped fresh dill, plus a few sprigs to garnish

1 tsp (5 mL) gin (optional)

salt, freshly ground pepper and sugar

**1** Cook pasta in boiling salted water until just *al dente*. Drain, rinse under cold water and drain again. Transfer to salad bowl and stir in a little vegetable oil.

**2** Season chicken breasts and cook them in butter until golden. Cool, then slice into strips and add to the pasta.

**3** Cut out the flesh of the honeydew using a melon baller, and add melon to the salad bowl along with the shrimp and celery.

**4** TO PREPARE DRESSING: Mix mayonnaise, yogurt, cream, chili sauce, dill and gin together and season to taste with salt, pepper and sugar. Pour over salad and toss lightly to coat. Cover with plastic wrap and chill for 1 hour or more before serving.

**SERVES 4 TO 6**

≈ HONEYDEW MELON

*Cantaloupe can be substituted for honeydew melon in this recipe*

# TAGLIATELLE AND BROAD BEANS

½ lb (225 g) shelled fresh young broad beans

1 tbsp (15 mL) olive oil

2 cloves garlic

¼ lb (110 g) pancetta or bacon, diced

1 lb (450 g) fresh tagliatelle or ⅔ lb (300 g) dried

1 stalk celery, sliced

1 tsp (5 mL) Dijon-style mustard

1 tbsp (15 mL) finely chopped fresh parsley

salt and freshly ground black pepper

juice of ½ lemon

1 tbsp (15 mL) extra virgin olive oil

½ lb (225 g) Parmigiano Reggiano (best quality Parmesan cheese), cut into ½ inch (1 cm) cubes

**1** Cook beans in boiling water until *al dente*, about 2 minutes, depending on their freshness. Drain, rinse under cold water and drain again. When cool enough to handle, peel the skins off; then set aside.

**2** Heat oil in a frying pan and sauté garlic cloves and pancetta until pancetta is crisp and light brown.

**3** Begin cooking tagliatelle in boiling salted water.

**4** To the frying pan add celery, mustard, parsley, salt and pepper. Stir and cook for 1 minute. Remove garlic cloves from the pan and add broad beans, lemon juice and extra virgin olive oil. Stir.

**5** When pasta is *al dente* drain and add to the pan with Parmesan. Toss briefly before transferring to individual plates.

**6** Serve with freshly grated Parmesan cheese and the pepper mill.

**SERVES 4 AS AN ENTRÉE OR LIGHT MAIN COURSE**

# SMOKED TROUT WITH FUSILLI

1 lb (450 g) fresh fusilli or ⅔ lb (300 g) dried

3 tbsp (45 mL) olive oil

2 tbsp (30 mL) finely chopped leek

1⅔ cups (415 mL) canned Italian peeled tomatoes

large pinch nutmeg

¼ tsp (1 mL) ground black pepper

¾ cup (185 mL) cream

salt

½ cup (125 mL) brandy

½ lb (225 g) smoked trout fillets, sliced into ¾ inch (2 cm) pieces

**LEMON PARMESAN CRUMBS**

3 tbsp (45 mL) grated Parmesan cheese

2 tsp (10 mL) dried bread crumbs

2 tsp (10 mL) finely chopped fresh parsley

rind of 1 lemon, grated

**1** Begin cooking fusilli in boiling salted water.

**2** In a frying pan, heat oil and cook leek gently until soft but not browned, about 3 minutes. Drain tomatoes and squeeze each one in your hand over the sink to remove excess juice and most of the seeds. Continue squeezing so that the pulp breaks up, then add to the leeks in the pan. Cover and cook over low heat for 3 to 4 minutes. Stir in nutmeg and black pepper. Add cream.

**3** Cook gently for another minute or two with the lid on. Taste for salt. Sometimes salt is not required, depending on the saltiness of the smoked trout.

**4** Drain pasta when it is three-quarters done and add to the sauce with brandy. Now turn up the heat and cook, stirring often, until the sauce is slightly thickened. Toss in trout and stir until heated through, 20 seconds or so.

**5 TO PREPARE LEMON PARMESAN CRUMBS:** Combine ingredients and mix well. Serve in a separate bowl.

**SERVES 4**

# GREEN SALAD PRIMAVERA

½ lb (225 g) fresh spinach fusilli, rotelli or other shape, or ⅓ lb (150 g) dried

1½ cups (325 mL) shelled fresh green peas

¼ lb (110 g) small green beans, both ends trimmed, cut in half

½ lb (225 g) fresh asparagus, cut into 1½ inch (4 cm) lengths

½ lb (225 g) broccoli florets

2 small zucchini, sliced diagonally

few sprigs fresh tarragon, to garnish

### DRESSING

¼ cup (60 mL) olive oil

2 tbsp (30 mL) fresh lemon juice

1 tsp (5 mL) Dijon-style mustard

1 tbsp (15 mL) finely chopped fresh tarragon or ½ tsp (2.5 mL) dried, crumbled and steeped in 1 tsp (5 mL) olive oil for 45 minutes

salt and freshly ground black pepper

**1** Cook pasta in boiling salted water until just *al dente*. Drain, rinse under cold water and drain again. Transfer to a bowl and stir in a little olive oil to keep it from sticking together.

**2** Separately blanch all the vegetables until tender-crisp; drain, rinse under very cold water and drain again. Add to pasta.

**3 TO PREPARE DRESSING:** Combine all ingredients. Pour over vegetables and toss lightly to coat. Decorate with tarragon sprigs. Can be served immediately, but is best if refrigerated for 1 to 2 hours first.

**SERVES 5 TO 6 AS A LIGHT MEAL**

*Green Salad Primavera*

*This light lasagna has a delicate flavor made possible only by using fresh basil; an interesting variation is to use purple basil.*

*Ricotta and Basil Lasagna*

# RICOTTA AND BASIL LASAGNA

1 lb (450 g) fresh lasagna sheets or ¾ lb (340 g) dried

¼ cup (60 mL) butter

3 tbsp (45 mL) all-purpose flour

salt and white pepper

pinch nutmeg

2 cups (500 mL) milk

1 tbsp (15 mL) finely chopped fresh basil

½ cup (125 mL) ricotta cheese

½ cup (125 mL) grated Parmesan cheese

1 tbsp (15 mL) extra chopped fresh basil

**1** In a pan of boiling salted water cook the lasagna sheets, a few at a time, until *al dente*.

Take out with a slotted spoon and dry between tea towels. It is necessary to precook the pasta sheets as the lasagna isn't in the oven long enough to steam them.

**2** Melt butter in a saucepan and stir in flour. Add a little salt, pepper and nutmeg and cook over low heat until it starts to change color. Stir in milk, a little at a time, and continue stirring until smooth and thickened. Remove from the heat and stir in 1 tbsp (15 mL) basil, the ricotta and half the Parmesan. Check seasonings.

**3** Preheat oven to 400°F (200°C).

**4** In a greased ovenproof dish place a sheet of pasta, followed by a thin layer of ricotta mixture. Sprinkle this with Parmesan and extra basil. Continue to layer in this order, finishing with the last of the sauce and Parmesan.

**5** Bake for just 20 minutes and serve hot.

**SERVES 4 TO 5 AS AN ENTRÉE**

# TUNA AND SPINACH ROTOLO

### PASTA

2½ cups (625 mL) all-purpose flour

large pinch salt

3 eggs, beaten

### FILLING

2½ lbs (1.2 kg) fresh spinach

9 oz (250 g) canned tuna in olive oil, drained and flaked

6 to 8 anchovy fillets, finely chopped

½ cup (125 mL) grated Parmesan cheese

1 cup (250 mL) fine white fresh bread crumbs

3 eggs, beaten

salt and freshly ground black pepper

**1 TO PREPARE PASTA:** Pile flour and salt onto a work surface and make a well in the center. Add eggs and begin to incorporate them into the flour, using a fork. When you have loosely united dough, use your hands

and begin kneading, adding a little flour or water if necessary as you go. Continue until the dough is smooth and elastic, about 6 minutes. Cover with a damp cloth or a piece of plastic wrap and let stand for 30 minutes.

**2 To Prepare Filling:** Remove stems from spinach leaves and discard. Rinse leaves under cold water and shake off excess water. Place in a large pot with a good pinch of salt and cook, covered, over low heat until leaves are wilted and tender. Drain and cool slightly. Squeeze out any excess water and chop spinach finely. Put in a large bowl and add tuna, anchovies, Parmesan, bread crumbs, eggs, a little salt and lots of black pepper. Mix thoroughly.

**3 To Assemble:** Using a rolling pin, roll out the dough to a large, even rectangle ⅛ inch (3 – 4 mm) thick. Place on a lightly floured cloth. Spread the filling over the dough, leaving 1¼ inches (3 cm) around the edges. Roll up the dough, jelly roll fashion, using the cloth to help lift and roll smoothly. Firmly wrap the roll in a thin layer of cheesecloth and tie off the ends securely with string. Place in a long narrow ovenproof pan, cover with lightly salted cold water and bring to the boil. Lower the heat and simmer for 15 to 20 minutes. Allow the rotolo to cool slightly in the cooking water before removing. Carefully take off the cloth and cut into slices for serving.

### SERVES 6

≈ **STUFFED PASTA ROLLS**

*Stuffed pasta rolls can be presented in several different ways. The slices can be arranged down a long shallow serving dish and topped with a hot light sauce such as fresh tomato; or they can be placed in a buttered ovenproof dish, sprinkled with Parmesan and butter and placed under the broiler for 5 minutes. For a milder flavor and slightly crisper texture, pour melted butter over the uncut roll and pop into a hot oven for 4 to 5 minutes. Rotolos make an eye catching buffet dish and are ideal served as an elegant appetizer or for a light lunch.*

# PENNE AND FRESH TUNA WITH RAISIN AND ALMOND SAUCE

**2 tbsp (30 mL) butter**

**1½ lbs (680 g) fresh tuna steaks, cut into strips**

**⅔ lb (300 g) penne**

**2 egg yolks, beaten**

### SAUCE

**⅓ cup plus 1 tbsp (100 mL) butter**

**3 tbsp (45 mL) all-purpose flour**

**¼ tsp (1 mL) nutmeg**

**salt and white pepper**

**1 cup (250 mL) white wine**

**3 tbsp (45 mL) currants**

**⅓ cup (85 mL) raisins**

**¼ cup (60 mL) blanched almonds, slivered**

**1 tbsp (15 mL) fresh lemon juice**

**1 tsp (5 mL) sugar**

**1** Melt butter in a large pan and gently sauté tuna until cooked through. Transfer to a plate and keep warm.

**2 To Prepare Sauce:** Melt butter and stir in flour. Cook, stirring, until the roux is smooth and golden. Add nutmeg, salt and pepper to taste and cook briefly. Gradually pour in wine, stirring constantly.

**3** When the sauce is smooth, stir in currants, raisins, almonds, lemon juice and sugar, bring to the boil and simmer over low heat for 20 minutes.

**4** Cook penne in boiling salted water.

**5** Whisk a little of the hot sauce into the egg yolks, then, with the saucepan off the stove, whisk the egg yolk mixture back into the sauce; keep warm.

**6** Drain penne when it is *al dente* and stir in a little vegetable oil; transfer to warmed plates.

**7** Top the pasta with pieces of tuna, then pour on sauce and serve, allowing guests to do the tossing.

### SERVES 4

≈ **PENNE AND FRESH TUNA WITH RAISIN AND ALMOND SAUCE**

*Here the rich, gamy flavor of tuna is nicely balanced by dried fruit and nuts. To vary, use a white-fleshed fish such as cod or sole, and omit the currants and raisins. Double the amount of almonds and toast them in the butter before making the roux.*

≈ **Tomato Fettuccine with Calamari and Snow Peas**

*A mild but rich sauce, this can be varied by omitting the cream and tossing the cooked pasta with the sauce in the pan before serving. It works as well using plain fettuccine and tossing with slivers of tomatoes at the end.*

# SCALLOPS AND ROASTED PEPPERS WITH TAGLIERINI

*If time is pressing, this sauce can be made quickly by substituting canned or bottled pimientos for the roasted pepper.*

**1 lb (450 g) fresh taglierini or ⅔ lb (300 g) dried**

**1 red pepper**

**1 green pepper**

**1 lb (450 g) fresh scallops, trimmed and cleaned**

**salt and freshly ground black pepper**

**all-purpose flour**

**3 tbsp (45 mL) olive oil**

**1 clove garlic**

**2 tsp (10 mL) chopped fresh parsley**

**juice of ½ lemon**

**2 leeks, white part only, thinly sliced**

**1 cup (250 mL) chicken stock**

**3 tbsp (45 mL) toasted fresh bread crumbs mixed with grated rind of 1 lemon**

**1** Roast peppers under the broiler until charred and blistered on all sides. Remove from heat and place in a plastic bag, sealed, to sweat. Remove when cool; peel and seed them, then slice into strips.

**2** Season scallops and coat them in flour. Heat oil, add garlic and quickly sauté scallops until just brown. Remove from the pan and sprinkle with parsley and lemon juice. Remove garlic clove.

**3** Add leeks to the pan and gently sauté until soft. Pour in stock, increase the heat slightly and reduce by half. Add scallops and pepper to the leeks and heat through.

**4** Cook pasta in boiling salted water until *al dente*. Drain and add to the sauce. Stir to coat and adjust seasoning if necessary. Serve at once, sprinkled with the lemon bread crumbs.

**Serves 4**

# SEAFOOD AGNOLOTTI WITH CORIANDER AND ZUCCHINI

**Pasta**

**3¼ cups (875 mL) all-purpose flour**

**large pinch salt**

**4 eggs**

**Filling**

**½ lb (225 g) white fish fillets (sole, ocean perch, halibut or haddock), poached, boned and finely chopped**

**½ lb (225 g) cooked shrimp or crab meat, finely chopped**

**2 tbsp (30 mL) finely chopped fresh coriander**

**⅔ cup (165 mL) fresh bread crumbs**

**⅓ cup (85 mL) finely grated fontina cheese**

**¼ tsp (2.5 mL) salt**

**¼ cup (60 mL) cooked spinach, wrung dry and finely chopped**

**1¾ cups (440 mL) ricotta**

**1 egg, beaten, to seal pasta**

**Sauce**

**⅓ cup (85 mL) butter**

**1 small zucchini, grated**

**salt and nutmeg**

**fresh coriander leaves, cut into thin strips, to garnish**

**1 To Prepare Pasta:** Pile flour on a work surface, make a well in the center and add salt and eggs. Using a fork, break up eggs and begin to incorporate flour. Continue blending in flour until you have a loosely formed mass of dough. Begin kneading with your hands, adding more flour or a little water if needed. Knead until you have a smooth, elastic ball. Wrap in damp cloth or plastic wrap and let stand for 30 minutes.

**2** Divide the ball into four, then, using a rolling pin or a hand-cranked pasta machine, roll out each one in turn to a very thin, even sheet. Let stand, covered, for 12 to 15 minutes.

**3 TO PREPARE FILLING:** Combine all filling ingredients, except beaten egg, in a bowl and mix well.

**4** Using a cookie cutter or the rim of a glass, cut out circles about 2 inches (5 cm) in diameter from the sheets of pasta, keeping pasta and circles you are not working on covered to prevent drying out. Working a few at a time, paint around the rim of each circle with beaten egg, place a little filling in the center and fold over to form a half-moon shape. Press the side together and go around the cut edges with a zigzag pastry wheel or a crimper cutter. As the agnolotti are completed, place them in a single layer and dust very lightly with flour. Simmer the agnolotti in boiling salted water for 3 to 4 minutes.

**5 TO PREPARE SAUCE:** Melt butter in a saucepan until golden, then add zucchini. Stir over very low heat, season with a little salt and a pinch of nutmeg and keep warm.

**6** Drain agnolotti, transfer to a warm serving dish, add sauce and stir. Sprinkle with sliced coriander and stir again before serving.

**SERVES 4**

# TOMATO FETTUCCINE WITH CALAMARI AND SNOW PEAS

½ lb (225 g) young calamari (squid), cleaned and cut into rings

milk

¾ lb (340 g) fresh tomato fettuccine or ⅔ lb (300 g) dried

3 tbsp (45 mL) unsalted butter

dash cognac or brandy

10 small snow peas, both ends trimmed, halved

salt and white pepper

1 to 2 pinches pure saffron powder

¾ cup (185 mL) cream

**1** Cover calamari rings with milk and soak for 45 minutes.

**2** Cook fettuccine in boiling salted water.

**3** Drain calamari, reserving milk, and fry quickly in melted butter until tender, 1 to 2 minutes. Add cognac and cook, stirring, until liquid is reduced. Add ¼ cup (60 mL) of the soaking milk and reduce liquid slightly before adding the snow peas. Season with salt and pepper and add saffron, then cook briefly before adding cream. Heat until slightly thickened.

**4** When fettuccine is *al dente*, drain, then transfer to warm plates. Spoon sauce over pasta then serve. Let guests toss their own.

**SERVES 4 ENTRÉES**

*Tomato Fettuccine with Calamari and Snow Peas (above) and Seafood Agnolotti with Coriander and Zucchini (below)*

# SAFFRON PASTA WITH SCALLOPS AND BLACK CAVIAR

### PASTA

1½ tsp (7.5 mL) pure saffron powder

2 tsp (10 mL) warm water

2½ cups (625 mL) all-purpose flour, or
1¼ cups (310 mL) all-purpose flour and
1 cup (250 mL) semolina

large pinch salt

3 eggs

### SAUCE

¾ lb (340 g) fresh scallops, soaked in milk
to cover for 30 minutes

2 tbsp (30 mL) butter

salt and white pepper

1 – 2 tsp (5 – 10 mL) Pernod or Ricard

1¼ cups (310 mL) cream

1 tbsp (15 mL) black caviar
or lumpfish caviar

**1 TO PREPARE PASTA:** Mix saffron in water and let stand for 10 minutes. Pile flour and salt onto a work surface and make a well in the center. Add eggs with saffron and water to the center and begin blending in the flours using a fork. When you have a roughly amalgamated dough, use your hands and knead until you have a smooth, elastic dough, adding more flour or water as necessary. Shape into a ball, wrap in plastic wrap or a damp cloth and let stand for 30 minutes. If preferred, the dough can be mixed in a food processor.

**2** Divide the dough into four balls. Working with one at a time, roll the balls out using a rolling pin or a hand-cranked pasta machine. When you have long, even sheets of tagliatelle thickness, cover again and let stand for at least 10 minutes. Then cut the pasta into tagliarini width, about ¼ inch (0.5 cm).

**3 TO PREPARE SAUCE:** Remove scallops from milk with a slotted spoon, reserving milk. Melt butter in a frying pan and fry scallops until just opaqaue. Season lightly and add Pernod. Turn up the heat and cook, stirring, until most of the liquid has evaporated. Remove scallops and set aside. Add cream to the pan and boil until thickened.

**4** Cook tagliarini in boiling salted water for 1½ to 2 minutes. Taste the sauce for salt and pepper, then stir in scallops and heat through. When pasta is *al dente*, drain and quickly stir in a little vegetable oil before distributing onto warmed plates. Spoon the sauce on top and then sprinkle with caviar; let the guests toss their own servings.

**SERVES 4 AS AN ENTRÉE**

# FRESH HERB FETTUCCINE WITH SMOKED SALMON AND ASPARAGUS

### PASTA

1⅔ cups (415 mL) all-purpose flour, or
1¼ cups (310 mL) all-purpose flour and
1 cup (250 mL) semolina

pinch salt

2 tsp (10 mL) finely chopped fresh parsley

2 tsp (10 mL) finely chopped fresh basil

2 eggs

### SAUCE

¾ lb (340 g) fresh asparagus spears,
trimmed, peeled and halved

2 tbsp (30 mL) butter

5 oz (150 g) sliced smoked salmon,
cut into strips

1 cup (250 mL) cream

freshly ground black pepper

**1 TO PREPARE PASTA:** Pile flour and salt on a work surface and make a well in the center. Add herbs and eggs and begin to incorporate into the flour, using a fork. When you have a loosely coherent dough, use your hands and knead it, adding a little flour or water if necessary, until it is smooth and elastic. Knead for at least 6 minutes and then let stand, covered with plastic wrap or a damp cloth, for 30 minutes.

**2** Divide the dough into two and roll each half out into a thin, even sheet using a rolling pin or a hand-cranked pasta machine. Let stand, covered, for 10 minutes before cutting the sheets into fettuccine. Set aside. Cover only if the pasta will have time to dry out and crack before cooking.

**3 TO PREPARE SAUCE:** In a large saucepan of boiling water put the bottom halves of the asparagus; boil for a minute before adding the tops and continue to cook until tender. Remove with a slotted spoon and rinse under cold water. Drain, and when cool enough to handle, cut each half in half again, discarding any woody sections. Top up the pan of water and bring back to the boil. Add fettuccine.

**4** In a large frying pan melt butter and add smoked salmon. Sauté gently for 30 seconds before adding cream. Increase the heat a little and cook to thicken, then add black pepper generously and toss in asparagus.

**5** When pasta is *al dente*, drain and transfer to the pan with sauce. Toss, then serve with freshly grated Parmesan and the pepper mill.

**SERVES 4 AS AN ENTRÉE**

### ≈ FRESH HERB PASTA

*Pasta flavored with fresh herbs makes a wonderful base for light, fresh sauces. Herbs and vegetables that are in season at the same time, like basil and asparagus in this recipe, often make perfect partners and require little else to flavor the dish. Along with the taste, the attractive appearance of green herbs through the pasta is reason enough to serve it with just melted butter and grated cheese. Try basil pasta with a cold sauce made from fresh ripe tomatoes, or fettuccine flavored with fresh sage coated with a creamy Gorgonzola sauce.*

# SWORDFISH WITH ZUCCHINI AND SAFFRON

**3 zucchini, julienned**

**3 tbsp (45 mL) unsalted butter**

**1 lb (450 g) fresh swordfish (or bonito or bluefin tuna) fillets, cut into 1¼ – 1½ inch (3 – 4 cm) slices**

**2 small onions, thinly sliced**

**1 clove garlic, crushed**

**pinch pure saffron powder**

**½ tsp (2.5 mL) salt**

**½ tsp (2.5 mL) freshly ground black pepper**

**½ cup (125 mL) chicken stock**

**½ cup (125 mL) cream**

**1 lb (450 g) fresh fettuccine or ¾ lb (340 g) dried**

**¼ tsp (1 mL) nutmeg**

**¼ tsp (1 mL) curry powder**

**1** Sprinkle zucchini with a little salt and let drain in a colander for 30 minutes.

**2** Melt half the butter in a large pan and fry swordfish until just cooked through. Remove with a slotted spoon and set aside.

**3** Add remaining butter to the pan and sauté onions and garlic until soft. Add saffron and seasonings and stir to coat. Add stock and cream and reduce over medium heat.

**4** Begin cooking the fettuccine in boiling salted water.

**5** When the sauce is smooth and thick, add drained zucchini and poach for 1 minute. Add swordfish and heat through.

**6** Drain pasta when it is *al dente*, transfer to a warm serving dish and pour the sauce over just before serving.

**SERVES 4 AS AN ENTRÉE OR LIGHT MEAL**

### ≈ SAFFRON

*Saffron comes from the autumn crocus flower. It can be bought in two forms: powdered or strands. The strands have to be steeped in a little water to draw out their flavor and color or can be lightly toasted to intensify the color.*

# SHELLS STUFFED WITH BACON, SPINACH AND RICOTTA

*To serve as an hors d'oeuvre, bake them at 350°F (180°C) until the cheese is golden; this tends to give a firmer textured pasta, which is easier to pick up with the fingers. Cook a couple more shells than you need, just in case one or two tear during cooking.*

**12 giant pasta shells**

**1 tsp (5 mL) olive oil**

**1 clove garlic, crushed**

**¼ lb (110 g) pancetta or bacon, cut into ½ inch (1 cm) pieces**

**4 canned Italian tomatoes**

**1 tbsp (15 mL) fresh bread crumbs**

**¼ cup (60 mL) cream**

**2¾ cups (685 mL) ricotta cheese**

**1 cup (250 mL) finely chopped, well-drained, cooked spinach**

**1 tsp (5 mL) chopped fresh basil or ½ tsp (2.5 mL) dried**

**3 tbsp (45 mL) grated Parmesan cheese**

**good pinch nutmeg**

**salt and freshly ground black pepper**

**extra grated Parmesan cheese**

**1** Cook pasta shells, stirring once or twice, until tender but firm. Drain, rinse under cold water and drain again. Set aside.

**2** Heat oil in a frying pan and sauté garlic and bacon until fat is extracted from the bacon and it becomes slightly crisp, 2 to 3 minutes.

**3** Squeeze tomatoes with your hand over the sink, shake off excess juice and add pulp to the pan. Stir in bread crumbs and fry briefly, then add cream. Cook for 1 to 2 minutes more, stirring well, until the mixture is quite dry.

**4** Place ricotta in a bowl with the bacon mixture, spinach, basil, Parmesan and nutmeg; mix well. Season with salt and pepper and a little more nutmeg if required.

*Shells Stuffed with Bacon. Spinach and Ricotta (above) and Pasta with Roasted Red Pepper*

**5** Stuff each pasta shell with some of the filling and place the shells close together in a shallow ovenproof dish.

**6** Sprinkle remaining filling and extra Parmesan over the top and place under a hot broiler until the cheese is melted and golden.

**SERVES 4 AS AN ENTRÉE**

# PASTA WITH ROASTED RED PEPPER

**5 large, deep red peppers**

**¾ lb (340 g) ridged pasta such as penne rigate, rotelli or conchiglie**

**3 tbsp (45 mL) extra virgin olive oil**

**3 tbsp (45 mL) olive oil**

**3 tbsp (45 mL) finely chopped fresh basil or ¼ cup (60 mL) fresh parsley**

**3 anchovy fillets, drained and finely minced**

**2 cloves garlic, crushed**

**salt and freshly ground black pepper**

**1** Place peppers under a hot broiler and roast them until the skins are charred and blistered. Turn them to make sure that the entire surface is black. Remove and place in a large plastic bag while still hot. Seal the bag and leave for 30 minutes, when the charred skins can be removed easily. Remove skins and seeds and slice peppers into 2 inch (5 cm) lengths. Sprinkle with a little of the extra virgin olive oil and set aside.

**2** Begin cooking pasta in boiling salted water.

**3** Heat olive oil in a frying pan and sauté basil, anchovies and garlic for 1 minute on low heat. Stir in peppers and season with salt and pepper. Add extra virgin olive oil and cook over low heat to develop the flavor.

**4** When pasta is *al dente*, drain and toss with sauce with a couple of roughly torn basil or parsley leaves.

**SERVES 4**

# SALMON WITH LEMON CANNELLONI

### TOMATO PASTA

2½ cups (625 mL) all-purpose flour

pinch salt

2 eggs

3 tbsp (45 mL) tomato paste

### FILLING

2 cups (500 mL) ricotta cheese

1¾ lbs (880 g) canned pink salmon, drained (reserve liquid)

juice of 1 lemon

1 large egg, lightly beaten

3 tbsp (45 mL) finely chopped onion

½ tsp (2.5 mL) salt

### SAUCE

¼ lb (110 g) butter

⅔ cup (165 mL) all-purpose flour

½ tsp (2.5 mL) salt

¼ tsp (1 mL) each white pepper and nutmeg

2¾ cups (685 mL) milk

reserved liquid from salmon

grated rind of 1 lemon

### GARNISH

1 tbsp (15 mL) chopped fresh dill

**1  TO PREPARE PASTA:** Sift flour and salt onto a work surface and make a well in the center. Lightly beat eggs with tomato paste and pour into flour well. Gradually work in flour using a fork until a roughly combined dough is formed. Then begin kneading to obtain a smooth dough. It may be necessary to incorporate extra flour if the dough is moist to the touch. Shape into a ball, cover with plastic wrap or an upturned bowl and let stand for 30 minutes.

**2**  Divide dough into two and roll each ball out into a thin, even sheet using a rolling pin or a hand-cranked pasta machine. Trim into rectangles about 5 x 5 inches (12 x 12 cm) or larger.

**3  TO PREPARE FILLING:** Place all ingredients in a bowl and combine well.

**4  TO PREPARE SAUCE:** Melt butter in a saucepan and stir in flour. Cook gently over low heat until smooth and slightly colored. Stir in salt, pepper and nutmeg. Gradually pour in milk, stirring constantly, and cook until smooth and thick. Add reserved salmon liquid and lemon rind and set aside to cool.

**5**  Preheat oven to 350°F (180°C).

**6  TO ASSEMBLE CANNELLONI:** Cook the pasta sheets, a couple at a time, in boiling salted water until *al dente*. Remove with a large slotted spoon and layer on dry tea towels to drain. Trim edges to desired size. Put a thick line of filling along the length of each sheet and roll up to make filled tubes. Spread one-third of the sauce over the bottom of a shallow ovenproof dish, then set the cannelloni tubes side by side in the dish. Pour remaining sauce over the top, covering all exposed pasta. Sprinkle with chopped dill and bake until bubbly, about 30 minutes.

**SERVES 4 AS AN ENTRÉE OR LIGHT MEAL**

# GORGONZOLA AND WALNUT RAVIOLI

### PASTA

3½ cups (875 mL) all-purpose flour

large pinch salt

4 eggs, lightly beaten

### FILLING

1 cup (250 mL) ricotta cheese

⅓ cup (85 mL) Gorgonzola cheese

½ cup (125 mL) walnuts, chopped

½ cup (125 mL) Parmesan cheese, grated

3 tbsp (45 mL) toasted fresh bread crumbs

1 egg, beaten, to seal pasta

### SAUCE

3 tbsp (45 mL) butter

½ cup (125 mL) cream

grated Parmesan cheese

1 **To Prepare Pasta:** Sift flour and salt into a pile on a work surface, making a well in the middle. Add eggs and begin to incorporate the flour, using a fork. Continue until you have a loosely blended dough. Using your hands, knead the dough until a smooth and elastic ball forms, about 6 minutes. Cover with plastic wrap or a damp cloth and let stand for 30 minutes.

2 Divide dough into four pieces. Working with one piece at a time, roll out to a very thin, even sheet, using a rolling pin or a hand-cranked pasta machine. Rest the sheets of pasta, covered, while you make the filling.

3 **To Prepare Filling:** Combine all ingredients except egg in a food processor or blender and mix until a coarse paste is obtained.

4 Working with 1 sheet of pasta at a time, cut out 2 x 2 inch (5 x 5 cm) squares and put a little filling in the center of each. Paint around the rims with beaten egg, then fold over diagonally to form triangles and press the cut edges together. Trim the cut edge with a zigzag pastry wheel or a crimper cutter, then put aside in a single layer until all are completed.

5 Add a few drops of olive oil to a large pot of boiling salted water. Poach the ravioli, a few at a time, until done, about 4 minutes. Transfer to a warm serving dish.

6 **To Prepare Sauce:** Melt butter, add cream and simmer until slightly thickened. Pour over ravioli, add 1½–2½ tbsp (20–40 mL) Parmesan, and toss lightly before serving. Serve with extra Parmesan and the pepper mill.

**SERVES 4**

# PORK AND VEAL TERRINE

¼ lb (110 g) ditalini or other very small pasta

1 small green pepper, seeded and roughly chopped

1 cup (250 mL) peeled and sliced carrots

4 cloves garlic

2 onions, roughly chopped

3 tbsp (45 mL) chopped fresh parsley

8 slices bacon

1½ tsp (8 mL) dried thyme

3 lbs (1.5 kg) ground pork and veal

¾ cup (185 mL) fresh bread crumbs

2 eggs, lightly beaten

1 tsp (5 mL) nutmeg

salt and freshly ground black pepper

1 Cook pasta in boiling salted water until *al dente*. Drain and rinse under cold water, then drain again.

2 Preheat oven to 350°F (180°C).

3 Put pepper, carrot, garlic, onion and parsley into a food processor or blender and process until they are chopped finely, almost a purée. Transfer mixture into a large bowl.

4 Finely chop 2 bacon slices by hand and add them to the bowl with thyme, ground meat, bread crumbs and eggs. Combine lightly, then add nutmeg, generous shaking of salt and pepper, and lastly the pasta. Mix well so that all the ingredients are evenly distributed.

5 Shape into a fat log and wrap loosely but evenly with remaining bacon slices. Place in a shallow baking dish and bake for 1½ hours.

**SERVES 6 TO 8**

≈ **PORK AND VEAL TERRINE**

*This loaf is as good cold as hot so it's an ideal choice for a picnic. It keeps well and slices beautifully because a tasty crust forms during baking.*

≈ CHOCOLATE

*In some parts of Spain, chocolate is often used to flavor fish dishes. Only a little is used, but the resulting sauce has a smooth mellow taste. There is a theory that this practice originated when Spanish sailors first brought chocolate to Europe.*

*Chicken Rolls with Paglia e Fieno*

# SPANISH STYLE FRESH TUNA AND LASAGNETTE

**1 tbsp (15 mL) olive oil**

**1⅓ lbs (600 g) fresh tuna, swordfish or other member of the tuna family**

**2 oz (55 g) prosciutto or unsmoked bacon, chopped**

**½ cup (125 mL) white wine**

**3 medium-size onions, cut in quarters**

**2 cloves garlic, cut in half**

**¾ lb (340 g) lasagnette, broken in half**

**1 tbsp (15 mL) grated unsweetened chocolate**

**1 tbsp (15 mL) dried bread crumbs**

**1 cup (250 mL) veal stock**

**few celery leaves, to garnish**

**1**  Put olive oil in the bottom of a large pot, add tuna and top with bacon, wine, onions and garlic. Cook over medium heat for 5 minutes, turn the tuna and cook for another 5 minutes. Lower heat and cook, covered, for 1½ to 2 hours.

**2**  Cook lasagnette in boiling salted water twenty minutes before serving.

**3**  Remove fish from the pot and keep warm. To the pot add chocolate, bread crumbs and stock. Stir them into the wine sauce and bring to the boil. Simmer for 4 to 5 minutes, then strain through a fine sieve. If a thicker sauce is desired, transfer it to a smaller saucepan and reduce quickly.

**4**  When pasta is *al dente*, drain and transfer to a warm serving dish. Top with pieces of fish, add sauce and serve with celery leaves scattered on top.

**SERVES 4**

# CHICKEN ROLLS WITH PAGLIA E FIENO

4 chicken fillets

¼ lb (110 g) prosciutto or raw smoked ham, finely chopped

3½ tbsp (50 mL) butter, softened

6 canned artichoke hearts, drained and quartered

salt and freshly ground black pepper

all-purpose flour

3 tbsp (45 mL) olive oil

1 small onion, finely chopped

½ cup (125 mL) dry white wine

⅔ cup (165 mL) chicken stock

1 lb (450 g) mixed fresh spinach and plain fettuccine or ⅔ lb (300 g) dried

2 to 3 sprigs fresh bay or lemon leaves, to garnish

Parmesan cheese, to serve

**1** Flatten each chicken fillet with a mallet, being careful not to tear the flesh. Mix prosciutto with half the butter and spread this mixture over the chicken slices. Top each with sections of artichoke hearts, season, and then roll up around the stuffing and secure tightly with string or skewers. Season rolls lightly and coat with flour; set aside.

**2** Heat remaining butter and olive oil in a casserole dish and gently sauté onion for 5 minutes. Add chicken rolls and fry, turning, until brown on all sides. Add wine, season to taste and cook briefly to reduce liquid a little. Lower the heat and cook, covered, for about 30 minutes or until meat is tender. From time to time add some chicken stock to maintain liquid, and adjust seasoning if necessary.

**3** Put fettuccine on to cook in boiling salted water. When *al dente*, drain and stir in a little olive oil. Transfer to warm serving dish. Stir in liquid from the chicken.

**4** Remove the skewers or string from the chicken rolls, arrange them on top of the pasta and decorate the dish with bay or lemon leaves. Serve immediately with freshly grated Parmesan.

**SERVES 4**

# TAGLIATELLE WITH ASPARAGUS, HAM AND CREAM

1 lb (450 g) fresh asparagus

salt

1 lb (450 g) fresh tagliatelle or ⅔ lb (300 g) dried

3½ tbsp (50 mL) butter

½ lb (225 g) prosciutto or unsmoked ham, cut into 1¼ inch (3 cm) strips

1 cup (250 mL) cream

freshly ground black pepper

3 tbsp (45 mL) freshly grated Parmesan cheese

**1** Put a large pan of water on to boil.

**2** Peel asparagus and discard tough bottoms. Cut the tip of each spear off about 1½ inches (4 cm) down, but keep stalk in one piece.

**3** Salt boiling water, add asparagus stalks, thickest ones first, and boil until half done. Add tips and continue boiling until tender but still crisp, stiff and bright green. Test as you go along. Remove from the water with a slotted spoon and cool slightly.

**4** Into the boiling water put the pasta. Melt butter in frying pan and add prosciutto. Fry until the butter begins to brown, but don't let the prosciutto become crisp. Add cream and bring to the boil, lifting up the bits off the pan bottom while stirring. Add a few good grinds from the pepper mill.

**5** Slice asparagus stalks into 1½ inch (4 cm) lengths, discarding any tough bottoms. Add to the sauce with the tops and stir to coat; the cream should have reduced and thickened.

**6** Drain pasta when it is *al dente* and pour into a warm serving bowl. Stir in the sauce and the Parmesan, toss to coat, and taste for salt and pepper before serving.

**SERVES 4**

≈ **CHICKEN ROLLS WITH PAGLIA E FIENO**

*This dish looks splendid and is a great hit when served for supper; the chicken rolls can be prepared earlier in the day, leaving only the pasta for last-minute cooking.*

≈ **TAGLIATELLE WITH ASPARAGUS, HAM AND CREAM**

*Asparagus, Parmesan, butter and black pepper: there's no better combination of flavors and I can't think of any way to improve this dish, unless it is to beat an egg with the Parmesan and stir this in at the last minute.*

≈ **ITALIAN TOMATOES**

*Italian peeled tomatoes are recommended because they are deep red and ripe, sweet and full of flavor, and they are canned in thick natural purée, which can be used elsewhere. Shop around and find the brand you like.*

# BAKED TORTELLINI WITH EGGPLANT AND POTATO

½ lb (225 g) eggplant, diced into ¾ inch (2 cm) pieces

½ lb (225 g) tortellini, filled with beef or cheese

½ lb (225 g) potatoes, peeled and cut into ¾ inch (2 cm) thick slices

½ cup (125 mL) olive oil

1 onion, thinly sliced

1⅔ cups (415 mL) canned Italian peeled tomatoes

½ tsp (2.5 mL) chopped fresh oregano or ¼ tsp (1 mL) dried

pinch cayenne pepper

salt and freshly ground black pepper

1 cup (250 mL) shredded fontina cheese

3 tbsp (45 mL) extra chopped fresh oregano or parsley

**1** Preheat oven to 375°F (150°C).

**2** Sprinkle eggplant with salt and leave to drain over the sink in a colander or strainer.

**3** Boil tortellini and when cooked drain and place in a shallow ovenproof dish.

**4** In a small saucepan, boil potatoes until just cooked. Drain. Heat some oil in a frying pan and sauté potatoes until brown, then add to the tortellini.

**5** With a little more oil, sauté onion gently for 5 minutes, then add drained eggplant. Continue cooking, adding more oil if necessary, until eggplant is tender and golden.

**6** Lightly drain tomatoes and add to the pan, breaking them up with a wooden spoon. Add oregano, cayenne, salt and pepper. Cook for 5 to 8 minutes more, or until the tomatoes have reduced and there is little liquid left.

**7** Add to the tortellini and toss with one-third of the fontina. Season again with a few grinds of black pepper and salt. Distribute the remaining fontina over the top and sprinkle with the extra oregano or parsley.

**8** Bake for 10 minutes, or until cheese melts and bubbles on top.

**SERVES 4**

# BUCATINI WITH TOMATOES AND SEAFOOD

1½ tbsp (20 mL) butter

1 tbsp (15 mL) olive oil

1 onion, finely chopped

3 cloves garlic, crushed

1 tsp (5 mL) finely chopped fresh parsley

good pinch thyme

5 cups (1.25 L) canned Italian peeled tomatoes, drained and puréed

salt and freshly ground black pepper

¾ cup (185 mL) fish stock or water

12 fresh or bottled baby clams, cleaned

5 oz (150 g) cleaned calamari (squid), sliced into rings

5 oz (150 g) uncooked shrimp meat, cut into pieces

5 oz (150 g) white fish fillets, cut into pieces

½ – 2 tsp (2.5 – 10 mL) turmeric, to taste

½ tsp (2.5 mL) pure saffron powder (optional)

dash Pernod or Ricard (optional)

1 lb (450 g) bucatini

**1** Melt butter and oil in a large pot and sauté onion and garlic over low heat for 5 minutes. Add parsley and thyme, stir, then add tomatoes. Season with salt and pepper, raise heat slightly and cook, covered, for 15 minutes.

**2** Remove the lid and cook for 5 to 10 minutes more, or until the sauce thickens. Add stock and bring to the boil. Add remaining ingredients and simmer until clams open and the seafood is cooked. Adjust seasoning. Discard any clams that have not opened.

**3** Cook bucatini in boiling salted water. When *al dente*, drain and transfer to a heated serving dish, then stir in the sauce. (Cheese is not usually served with seafood sauces.)

**SERVES 4**

*Baked Tortellini with Eggplant and Potato*

≈ OLIVE OIL

*Pure olive oil is chemically treated and blended, but only with other olive oils. It contains no cholesterol. Extra virgin olive oil is generally made from the first pressing of slightly underripe olives and is sometimes produced without chemical means.*

# BAKED EGGPLANT AND WHOLE-WHEAT FETTUCCINE

**1 lb (450 g) fresh whole-wheat fettuccine or ½ lb (225 g) dried**

**2 eggplants, cut into ½ inch (1 cm) slices**

**salt and freshly ground black pepper**

**⅓ cup (85 mL) olive oil**

**1 onion, chopped**

**1 clove garlic, crushed**

**1 lb (450 g) fresh tomatoes, peeled, seeded and chopped**

**2 tsp (10 mL) chopped fresh basil or 1 tsp (5 mL) dried**

**4 zucchini, sliced**

**2½ cups (625 mL) button mushrooms, sliced**

**3 tbsp (45 mL) wheat germ**

**3 tbsp (45 mL) chopped fresh parsley**

**½ lb (225 g) mozzarella cheese, sliced**

**½ cup (125 mL) cream**

**1** Break fettuccine into thirds and cook in boiling water until *al dente*. Drain and set aside with a little olive oil stirred in to prevent sticking.

**2** Lightly sprinkle eggplant slices with salt and let drain for 30 minutes.

**3** Heat half the oil in a saucepan and gently sauté onion and garlic for 5 minutes. Add tomatoes, basil, salt and pepper and simmer, uncovered, until the sauce has thickened, about 12 minutes.

**4** Preheat oven 350°F (180°C).

**5** Drain and dry eggplant. In a frying pan heat the remaining oil and sauté eggplant slices until golden; set aside. Fry zucchini, mushrooms and wheat germ until tender, and then combine with the eggplant.

**6** Arrange half the fettuccine in the bottom of a greased deep ovenproof dish. Sprinkle with half the parsley, then arrange half the eggplant mixture on top of the parsley. Pour half the tomato sauce over the eggplant. Repeat layering, then cover the last layer of tomatoes with the mozzarella slices. Pour cream over the top and bake, uncovered, for 30 minutes.

**SERVES 4 TO 6**

# TAGLIERINI WITH SARDINES

**1 small fennel bulb**

**12 fresh sardines, about 5 inches (12 cm) long, cleaned and split open**

**½ cup (125 mL) all-purpose flour, seasoned with salt and pepper**

**½ cup (125 mL) olive oil**

**1 small onion, finely chopped**

**1 anchovy fillet, chopped**

**3 tbsp (45 mL) toasted pine nuts**

**1 tbsp (15 mL) raisins**

**pinch pure saffron powder**

**freshly ground black pepper**

**1 lb (450 g) mixed fresh spinach and plain taglierini or ⅔ lb (300 g) dried**

**1** Chop the green beards from the fennel and reserve. Trim the bulb, discarding any tough outer stalks, and finely slice enough to make ¼ cup (60 mL). Save the rest for another use.

**2** Toss sardines in seasoned flour and fry them very gently in half the olive oil, a few at a time. Be careful not to break them when turning. Remove and keep warm.

**3** Heat the rest of the oil and fry onion and fennel until soft. Add anchovy and fry, mashing as you stir, for 30 seconds. Add pine nuts, raisins, saffron and a little black pepper. Stir and keep warm.

**4** Cook taglierini in boiling salted water until *al dente*. Drain and put in a warm serving dish. Add the fennel sauce, toss and place sardines on top. Sprinkle with fennel greens and serve immediately.

**SERVES 4**

# SPAGHETTI WITH CALAMARI

**1¾ lbs (800 g) fresh baby squid (calamari)**

**⅓ cup (85 mL) olive oil**

**1 large onion, finely chopped**

**3 cloves garlic, crushed**

**pinch chili flakes**

**2½ cups (625 mL) canned Italian peeled tomatoes, drained and chopped**

**salt and freshly ground black pepper**

**1⅓ lbs (600 g) fresh spaghetti or
1 lb (450 g) dried**

**3 tbsp (45 mL) chopped fresh coriander**

**1**  Remove head from squid and cut the tentacles straight across above the eyes. Discard head; keep tentacles and body, squeezing out the bony beak. If tentacles are a bit large, divide them into two. Remove the thin bone from the sacs and rinse the sacs under cold water. Peel off the outer thin skin of each sac, washing under cold water as you go. If you think the sacs are a little large, cut them into sections.

**2**  Heat oil and sauté onion, garlic and chili gently for 5 to 6 minutes, until onion is soft and golden.

**3**  Add squid and cook until it turns opaque. Add tomatoes and season well with salt and pepper. Stir well, then lower the heat and cook, covered, for 30 minutes.

**4**  Cook spaghetti in boiling salted water until *al dente*. Drain and transfer to a warm serving bowl. Add squid sauce and coriander and stir just before serving.

**SERVES 4**

# SPAGHETTI WITH CLAMS

**2 lbs (1 kg) small clams, washed and scrubbed**

**1 cup (250 mL) dry white wine**

**1 cup (250 mL) water**

**⅓ cup (85 mL) olive oil**

**2 cloves garlic, crushed**

**1 onion, finely chopped**

**3⅓ cups (835 mL) canned Italian peeled tomatoes, drained and chopped**

**3 tbsp (45 mL) finely chopped fresh parsley**

**pinch chili**

**3 tbsp (45 mL) butter**

**salt and freshly ground black pepper**

**1⅓ lbs (600 g) fresh spaghetti or
1 lb (450 g) dried**

**1**  Place clams in a large pan with wine, water and 1 tbsp (15 mL) oil. Cover and cook over high heat. As the clams open remove them with a slotted spoon; discard any that

don't open. Continue boiling the liquid until roughly 1 cup (250 mL) remains: strain through cheesecloth and set aside.

**2**  In a large pan heat remaining oil and sauté garlic and onion until golden. Add clam juice and let it evaporate a little before adding tomatoes, parsley, chili and butter. Cook, uncovered, for 10 minutes over medium heat. Season sauce and add a little more wine if it becomes too thick. Add clams and stir to heat.

**3**  Cook spaghetti in boiling salted water. When it is *al dente*, drain and stir in a little olive oil to prevent sticking.

**4**  Transfer to warm bowls, top with sauce and serve with a small slice of butter on top of each dish, but no cheese.

**SERVES 4**

*Spaghetti with Clams*

**≈ SPAGHETTI
WITH CLAMS**

*Other shellfish can be included in the sauce, and the chili can be left out if a less spicy dish is preferred. If only large clams are available, prepare them as below but remove the meat and discard most of the shells, saving just a few for decoration.*

# SHELLS AND SHELLFISH SALAD

**1 lb (450 g) medium-sized conchiglie**

**1⅓ cups (330 mL) mayonnaise, preferably homemade**

**¼ cup (60 mL) chopped fresh tarragon or 3 tbsp (45 mL) dried**

**1 tbsp (15 mL) finely chopped fresh parsley**

**cayenne pepper**

**fresh lemon juice**

**2 lbs (1 kg) cooked shellfish flesh: shrimp, lobster, crab or a combination, cut into bite-size pieces**

**2 mild red radishes, sliced**

**½ green pepper, julienned**

**salt and freshly ground black pepper**

**1** Cook pasta in boiling salted water until *al dente*. Drain, rinse under cold water and drain again. Place in a large bowl and stir in 1½–2½ tbsp (20–40 mL) mayonnaise.

*Shells and Shellfish Salad*

Cool to room temperature, stirring occasionally to prevent sticking.

**2** If using dried tarragon, simmer it in ¼ cup (60 mL) milk for 3 to 4 minutes; drain. Combine tarragon, parsley, cayenne, lemon juice and remaining mayonnaise and mix well.

**3** Add shellfish to pasta with most of the radishes and green pepper and the salt and pepper. Stir in the tarragon mayonnaise and toss gently to coat. Cover and chill before serving, adding more mayonnaise if the mixture is a little dry. Decorate with remaining radish and green pepper slices.

**SERVES 8 AS AN ENTRÉE, 4 AS A MAIN COURSE**

## ≈ PARSLEY

*The parsley with the best flavor and leaf is the flat-leafed Italian variety. Dried parsley is simply not a good alternative in any recipe requiring fresh parsley.*

# LASAGNA WITH SHRIMP AND ARTICHOKE HEARTS

3⅓ cups (835 mL) canned Italian peeled tomatoes, drained and pulped

1 clove garlic, crushed

salt and freshly ground black pepper

pinch chili flakes

½ tsp (2.5 mL) finely chopped fresh basil or ¼ tsp (1 mL) dried

¼ cup (60 mL) olive oil

½ lb (225 g) dried lasagna sheets or ⅔ lb (300 g) fresh

¾ lb (340 g) shelled cooked shrimp, halved if large

6 canned artichoke hearts, each cut into 6

3 tbsp (45 mL) chopped fresh parsley

¼ lb (110 g) mozzarella cheese, sliced

8 to 10 thin anchovy fillets

**1** Preheat oven to 400°F (200°C).

**2** Put tomatoes, garlic, salt, pepper, chili flakes, basil and olive oil in a shallow ovenproof dish. Stir to combine and bake for 25 to 30 minutes.

**3** While the tomato sauce is baking, cook lasagna sheets until *al dente*; drain and place on dry tea towels (do not layer).

**4** **TO ASSEMBLE LASAGNA:** Grease a rectangular ovenproof dish. Put a thin layer of tomato sauce on the bottom and cover with a single layer of pasta. Combine the rest of the tomato sauce with shrimp, artichoke hearts, parsley, salt and pepper. Now alternate layers of sauce and pasta, finishing with a layer of sauce. Cover with slices of mozzarella and top with a lattice pattern of anchovies.

**5** Lower heat to 350°F (180°C) and bake for 40 minutes, or until golden on top.

**SERVES 4**

# ROAST BEEF WITH ROTELLI

½ cup (125 mL) olive oil

3 tbsp (45 mL) butter

4½ lbs (2 kg) onions, thinly sliced

2 lb (1 kg) pot roast or brisket

¼ lb (110 g) diced pancetta or bacon

1 stalk celery, chopped

1 carrot, chopped

sprig fresh marjoram or ½ tsp (2.5 mL) dried

salt and freshly ground black pepper

1 cup (250 mL) dry white wine

3 tbsp (45 mL) water, beef stock or cream

1 lb (450 g) fresh rotelli or ¾ lb (340 g) dried

**1** Preheat oven to 300°F (150°C).

**2** Melt 3 tbsp (45 mL) oil and the butter in a large Dutch oven. Add onions and sauté over a low heat until golden and tender, at least 15 minutes. Transfer to a plate.

**3** Heat remaining oil in the Dutch oven and brown the roast on all sides. Add pancetta or bacon and fry for a short time before adding celery and carrot, marjoram, salt and pepper. Fry for 1 to 2 minutes then return onions to the Dutch oven with half the wine. Mix in the vegetables well and cook for 1 minute until the raw wine aroma dissipates, then cover the Dutch oven and transfer to the oven.

**4** Bake for 2 to 2½ hours or until the meat is tender. Add more wine as the juices reduce. A rich, dark gravy should surround the beef. Transfer the meat to a carving platter and keep warm.

**5** Pour off 1½ cups (375 mL) of the gravy and place in a blender or food processor with 3 tbsp (45 mL) water, beef stock or cream. Blend until you have a smooth, thick sauce. Transfer to a small saucepan to keep hot.

**6** Cook pasta in boiling salted water. Drain and serve with the onion sauce and grated Parmesan as the first course. Carve the beef and serve it with its gravy for the main course.

**SERVES 5 TO 6**

≈ **ROAST BEEF WITH ROTELLI**

*The beef is also delicious served with a hot fresh tomato sauce instead of the gravy. Yellow and green patty pan squash are an attractive vegetable to serve as an accompaniment; potatoes are not usually served with this dish.*

*This chicken is excellent served cold on a picnic. The flesh remains moist and succulent and the stuffing becomes a side salad. Those bacon slices that didn't burn during the roasting can be crumbled and used in other dishes, for example tossed through a green salad or used as flavoring in a pasta sauce.*

# ROAST CHICKEN WITH PASTA STUFFING

⅓ lb (150 g) small shaped dried pasta (pennete or ditali)

12 green onions, white parts only, thinly sliced

12 pistachio nuts, shelled

3 tbsp (45 mL) finely chopped mixed fresh herbs (parsley, basil, sage or oregano)

5 canned Italian peeled tomatoes, drained and pulped

1 slice bacon, cut into small pieces

¼ tsp (1 mL) salt

½ tsp (2.5 mL) freshly ground black pepper

3½ tbsp (50 mL) butter, softened

2 lbs (1 kg) fresh chicken

1 slice bread

4 extra bacon slices

**1** Cook pasta until three-quarters done then drain it.

**2** Preheat oven to 425°F (200°C).

**3** In a large bowl combine green onions, pistachio nuts, herbs, tomatoes, diced bacon, salt and pepper with the pasta.

**4** Using half the butter, grease the inside of the chicken and fill it with the pasta mixture. Place a slice of bread inside the opening to keep the stuffing in, fold flaps of skin over it and skewer tightly closed.

**5** Rub the chicken with the remaining butter and place it on its side on a rack in a baking dish. Sprinkle the chicken with a little ground black pepper and cover it with the extra bacon. Roast for 20 minutes.

**6** Turn the bird onto its other side, sprinkle with a little more ground black pepper, cover with the bacon and put back into the oven for 20 minutes more.

**7** Remove the bacon, turn the bird onto its back and roast again, basting often with the juices in the dish. After 20 minutes test to see if the chicken is cooked. If a skewer pushed into the thick flesh of a thigh produces liquid with a red tinge, roast the bird for another 5 minutes and test again. When the juices come clear it's time to take the chicken out. Let stand for a couple of minutes in a warm place before carving.

**SERVES 2 – 3**

# FUSILLI AND SNAPPER BAKED IN A PARCEL

¼ lb (110 g) fusilli

⅓ cup (85 mL) butter

1 clove garlic

1 red pepper, cut into strips

1⅓ lbs (600 g) snapper fillets or other white fleshed fish, cut into bite-size pieces

1¼ cups (310 mL) button mushrooms, sliced

2 tsp (10 mL) each chopped fresh parsley and fresh dill

salt and freshly ground black pepper

½ cup (125 mL) cream

3 tbsp (45 mL) dry white wine

**1** Cook fusilli in boiling salted water until not quite *al dente*. Drain and stir in a little vegetable oil to prevent sticking.

**2** In a frying pan melt butter and gently sauté garlic clove and red pepper for 2 minutes. Add snapper fillets and sauté until fish is just opaque. Add mushrooms, sauté briefly and then discard garlic. Stir in parsley and dill, season well and add cream. Cook until cream bubbles and then stir in the fusilli.

**3** Preheat oven to 400°F (200°C).

**4** Divide the mixture between four large sheets of aluminium foil or greased kitchen parchment. Season again lightly, sprinkle each with 2 tsp (10 mL) wine and fold up parcels, sealing well to keep steam from escaping. Place in a large shallow baking dish and bake for 20 minutes. Open carefully to let the steam out and serve immediately.

**SERVES 4**

## SPAGHETTI WITH LAMB AND RED PEPPER

**3 tbsp (45 mL) butter**

**3 tbsp (45 mL) olive oil**

**3 red peppers, cut into thin strips
1¼ – 1½ inches (3 – 4 cm) long**

**1 onion, finely chopped**

**3 cloves garlic, crushed**

**1 lb (450 g) lamb, diced**

**2 tsp (10 mL) vinegar**

**1⅔ cups (415 mL) canned Italian peeled
tomatoes, drained and chopped**

**¼ tsp (1 mL) chili flakes**

**salt**

**dry white wine**

**1⅓ lbs (600 g) fresh spaghetti or
1 lb (450 g) dried**

**½ cup (125 mL) grated pecorino cheese**

**1½ – 2½ tbsp (20 – 40 mL) finely chopped
fresh parsley**

**1** In a heavy-based casserole dish heat half the butter and oil and gently sauté red peppers for 5 minutes. Remove from the dish with a slotted spoon and set aside.

**2** Add remaining butter and oil to the dish and sauté onion, garlic and lamb over medium heat until the lamb is lightly browned. Stir in vinegar, cover and let stand for 10 minutes before proceeding.

**3** Add tomatoes, chili flakes and red peppers, season with salt and cook the sauce for 5 minutes. Lower the heat and cook, covered, for 30 minutes more, stirring once or twice. Add a little wine from time to time if the sauce begins to dry. Adjust seasoning if necessary.

**4** Cook spaghetti in boiling salted water until *al dente*. Drain and transfer to a warm serving dish. Pour sauce over spaghetti and add pecorino and parsley. Toss together lightly and serve with extra pecorino.

**SERVES 4 AS A MAIN COURSE**

**≈ RED PEPPERS**

*The darker the color, the sweeter they are, and the more concentrated the flavor, especially if broiled or roasted.*

**≈ PECORINO CHEESE**

*This was originally made from sheep's milk. It is sharper and more piquant than Parmesan.*

*Rigatoni with Sausage
and Fresh Marjoram*

# RIGATONI WITH SAUSAGE AND FRESH MARJORAM

**1½ tbsp (20 mL) butter**

**1 tbsp (15 mL) olive oil**

**1 onion, chopped**

**1 carrot, julienned**

**1 bay leaf**

**2½ oz (70 g) bacon, chopped**

**½ lb (225 g) spicy Italian sausage, skinned and sliced**

**1⅔ cups (415 mL) canned Italian peeled tomatoes**

**salt and freshly ground black pepper**

**½ cup (125 mL) beef or chicken stock**

**1 lb (450 g) rigatoni**

**1½ heaped tbsp (25 mL) chopped fresh marjoram or oregano**

**1** Heat butter and oil in a frying pan and cook onion and carrot with bay leaf until onion is transparent.

**2** Add bacon and sausage and cook, stirring often, until brown.

**3** Squeeze half the tomatoes dry over the sink, pulp the flesh with your hand and add to the pan. Add the rest whole and break up loosely with the spoon while stirring. Season well with salt and pepper and simmer for 30 minutes over low heat, gradually adding stock as sauce reduces.

**4** Cook rigatoni in boiling salted water until *al dente*. Drain and transfer to a warm serving dish. Add marjoram and sauce, and toss together lightly before serving.

**SERVES 4**

**≈ RIGATONI WITH SAUSAGE AND FRESH MARJORAM**

*The success of this sauce depends upon the quality of the sausages, and on fresh marjoram being used. The flavor is rich and spicy, and the appearance should be fresh and bright.*

# BAKED SNAPPER AND PENNE WITH CITRUS SAUCE

½ lb (225 g) penne

½ cup (125 mL) vegetable oil

4 small to medium snapper steaks or other white-fleshed fish, trimmed

2 to 3 cloves garlic, crushed

1 tbsp (15 mL) chopped fresh coriander, plus some sprigs for decoration

⅔ cup (165 mL) puréed fresh tomatoes or juice from canned Italian peeled tomatoes

¼ cup (60 mL) fresh citrus juice: lime, lemon, Seville orange, or a combination

chili flakes

**1** Cook penne in boiling salted water until barely *al dente*. Drain and stir in a little vegetable oil to prevent sticking. Transfer to an ovenproof dish.

**2** In a frying pan heat some of the oil and brown the snapper on both sides. Lay pieces of snapper side by side on top of the penne, covering it completely.

**3** Preheat oven to 425°F (220°C).

**4** In the frying pan heat remaining oil and gently sauté garlic. Add chopped coriander, then puréed tomato and citrus juice. Cook, stirring, until the sauce boils and gives off a citrus aroma.

**5** Sprinkle in chili flakes to taste, then pour sauce over snapper. Pour in a little water, about ¼ cup (60 mL), to make sure all the pasta is moistened. Cover loosely with foil and bake for 25 to 30 minutes, or until snapper is tender. Decorate with coriander sprigs and serve from the dish.

**SERVES 4**

# MEAT ROLL STUFFED WITH SPINACH AND HAM

### MEAT MIXTURE

2 lbs (1 kg) lean ground beef

2 eggs, beaten

1 tsp (5 mL) thyme

½ tsp (2.5 mL) each salt, black pepper and crushed garlic

1 onion, finely chopped

3 tbsp (45 mL) finely chopped fresh parsley

½ cup (125 mL) dried bread crumbs

½ cup (125 mL) Marsala

1 tsp (5 mL) tomato paste

### SPINACH MIXTURE

¾ cup (185 mL) well-drained, cooked spinach, finely chopped

2 oz (60 g) cooked stellini or other tiny interestingly shaped pasta

½ cup (125 mL) grated Cheddar cheese

¼ cup (60 mL) grated Parmesan cheese

¼ tsp (1 mL) each salt, pepper and nutmeg

¼ lb (110 g) ham, finely chopped

### TOPPING

¼ cup (60 mL) fresh bread crumbs mixed with ¼ cup (60 mL) grated Parmesan

**1 TO PREPARE MEAT MIXTURE:** Thoroughly combine ingredients in a bowl.

**2 TO PREPARE SPINACH MIXTURE:** Combine ingredients well in another bowl.

**3** Preheat oven to 350°F (180°C).

**4** To assemble the roll, on a large sheet of foil flatten meat mixture into a rectangle approximately ½ inch (0.5 cm) thick, 6 inches (15 cm) long and 3½ inches (9 cm) wide. Spread spinach mixture evenly over the top. Roll up, jelly roll fashion, starting at one of the shorter sides and using the foil to lift and roll.

**5** Sprinkle with topping and wrap loaf tightly in foil. Place in a small deep-sided baking dish and bake for 1½ hours. Let stand for 5 minutes, still in the foil, before serving.

**SERVES 6 TO 8**

≈ MEAT ROLL STUFFED WITH SPINACH AND HAM

*When served hot this loaf hardly requires a sauce as it is moist and succulent. Cold, it slices well for picnics and makes delicious sandwiches.*

## FONTINA CHEESE

*A soft, delicate cheese from the Piedmont region in Italy. It is slightly nutty and has good melting qualities.*

## PARMESAN CHEESE

*Wherever possible use Parmigiano Reggiano, the best quality Parmesan.*
*Parmesan cheese is low in fat with a very high protein content.*

# ZUCCHINI AND SAUSAGE LASAGNA

½ cup (125 mL) olive oil

2 small carrots, finely chopped

1 onion, finely chopped

2 stalks celery, finely chopped

½ lb (225 g) spicy sausages

⅔ cup (180 mL) dry white wine

3⅓ cups (835 mL) canned Italian peeled tomatoes, drained and chopped

salt and freshly ground black pepper

1¾ lbs (800 g) small zucchini, sliced

½ tsp (2.5 mL) chopped fresh oregano or ¼ tsp (1 mL) dried

1 lb (450 g) lasagna sheets

2 cups (500 mL) shredded fontina cheese

¾ cup (185 mL) grated Parmesan cheese

**1** Heat half the oil in a pan and add carrots, onion and celery. Fry gently until softened.
**2** Remove casings from sausages and discard. Add meat to the pan and break up with a wooden spoon when stirring. Fry until brown, then pour in wine. Increase heat and cook until liquid is reduced by half.
**3** Add tomatoes, lower heat and simmer for 40 minutes, stirring from time to time. Season to taste.
**4** In a separate pan, heat the remaining oil and fry zucchini with a little salt and oregano until tender and golden.
**5** Cook lasagna according to instructions and drain on dry tea towels.
**6** Preheat oven to 375°F (190°C).
**7** In a greased deep rectangular ovenproof dish place a layer of pasta. Add a thin layer of sauce, then some zucchini slices. Sprinkle with some fontina and Parmesan cheese. Continue this layering until all ingredients are used up, finishing with fontina and Parmesan. Bake for 30 minutes.

**SERVES 6 TO 8 AS A MAIN COURSE**

# TAGLIATELLE WITH VEAL, WINE AND CREAM

*Rich and filling, this dish makes an ideal meal served with a tossed salad. For a lighter sauce, the cream can be omitted and it's just as delicious.*

1 lb (450 g) veal scallopine or escalopes, cut into strips

flour seasoned with salt and pepper

3½ tbsp (50 mL) butter

1 onion, sliced

½ cup (125 mL) dry white wine

4 – 5 tbsp (60 – 75 mL) beef stock or chicken stock

⅔ cup (165 mL) cream

salt and freshly ground black pepper

1⅓ lbs (600 g) fresh tagliatelle or 1 lb (450 g) dried

freshly grated Parmesan cheese

**1** Coat pieces of veal with seasoned flour and fry quickly in melted butter until browned. Remove with a slotted spoon and set aside.
**2** Add onion to the pan and sauté gently until soft and golden, 8 to 10 minutes. Pour in wine and cook rapidly until the raw wine smell disappears, then add stock and cream and season with salt and pepper. Reduce again, then add veal.
**3** Cook tagliatelle in boiling salted water until *al dente*. Drain and transfer to a warm serving dish.
**4** Check the sauce for salt and pepper, stir in about 1 tbsp (15 mL) Parmesan, pour sauce on the pasta and toss. Serve with extra Parmesan.

**SERVES 4**

*Tagliatelle with Veal, Wine and Cream*

# ENDINGS

At the end of the day or the end of a meal, pasta works beautifully. With interesting textures and tastes of its own, it also provides the perfect foil for other flavors. In this section we have included recipes for luscious desserts, light suppers and delicious midnight snacks.

## PASTA SOUFFLÉ

**3 cups (750 mL) milk**

**grated rind of ½ small lemon**

**2 tsp (10 mL) salt**

**½ lb (225 g) dried spaghetti or tagliatelle**

**¼ cup plus 1 tbsp (75 mL) butter, softened**

**½ cup (125 mL) sugar**

**3 large eggs, separated**

**½ cup (125 mL) raisins soaked in ¼ cup (60 mL) brandy**

**¾ cup (185 mL) chopped blanched almonds**

**pinch ground cinnamon**

**1** Preheat oven to 375°F (200°C).

**2** Put milk, lemon rind and salt in a large saucepan and bring to the boil. Add pasta and gently cook, covered, until the pasta is tender, about 8 minutes. Remove the lid and set the pan in cold water to cool.

**3** Cream butter and sugar together until smooth and light. Add egg yolks one at a time, beating well after each addition. Stir in milk and pasta, raisins and brandy, almonds and cinnamon.

**4** Beat egg whites until stiff and loosely fold into the pasta mixture. Turn into a large buttered soufflé dish and bake for 45 to 60 minutes. The top should be lightly browned and the center set or, if you prefer, slightly custardy.

**SERVES 4 TO 6**

≈ **SWEET PASTA CAKE**

*Served cold, this cake is a great finale to a picnic or barbecue; served warm with mascarpone or cream at a dinner party, it is quite special.*

---

## ≈ PASTA AND FRESH FRUIT WITH YOGURT

*This is a delicious dessert. Cook ⅔ lb (300 g) small conchiglie until just al dente. Drain and rinse in cold water. Stir in 1 tsp (5 mL) oil and cool. Sprinkle a selection of fresh fruit (melon, kiwi fruit, peaches, mixed berries) with some fresh orange juice and lemon juice and a little sugar. Chill. Mix some yogurt with honey, vanilla and Cointreau. Toss with pasta to coat. Pile pasta up on a large plate and surround with fruit. Decorate with toasted almonds and fresh mint leaves.*

---

# SWEET PASTA CAKE

**⅔ lb (300 g) fresh spaghetti or ½ lb (225 g) dried**

**2 tbsp (30 mL) butter**

**3 tbsp (45 mL) sugar**

**⅓ cup (85 mL) mixed candied peel**

**⅓ cup (85 mL) raisins**

**¼ cup (60 mL) almonds**

**¼ cup (60 mL) chopped dried figs or dates**

**3 tbsp (45 mL) glacé cherries, chopped**

**3 tbsp (45 mL) all-purpose flour**

**½ tsp (2.5 mL) cinnamon**

**2 eggs, beaten**

**1** Cook pasta in boiling salted water until *al dente*. Drain, rinse under cold water and drain again. Transfer to a bowl.

**2** Preheat oven to 350°F (180°C).

**3** Melt butter in a small saucepan. Add sugar and heat, stirring, until sugar dissolves. Leave to cool.

**4** In a large bowl, combine peel, raisins, almonds, figs, glacé cherries, flour and cinnamon. Mix well, then stir in pasta and add butter-sugar mixture and eggs. Toss to coat.

**5** Transfer mixture to a greased 8 inch (20 cm) pie plate and level it out. Bake until set and golden on top, about 35 minutes. If the top browns too much, cover loosely with foil. When done, remove from oven and let stand for 20 minutes before turning out of pie plate.

**SERVES 6 TO 8**

# CHESTNUT AGNOLOTTI

**1½ lbs (680 g) moist fresh pasta sheets, thinly rolled**

### FILLING

**1 lb (450 g) chestnut purée**

**3 tbsp (45 mL) honey**

**3 tbsp (45 mL) cocoa powder**

**3 tbsp (45 mL) ground almonds**

**1 tsp (5 mL) cinnamon**

**1 tsp (5 mL) vanilla extract**

**2 tsp (10 mL) rum**

**¼ cup (60 mL) finely chopped mixed candied peel**

**¾ cup (185 mL) fresh bread crumbs**

**1 tbsp (15 mL) sugar**

### TO ASSEMBLE

**beaten egg for sealing**

**vegetable oil for frying**

**melted honey and icing sugar, to finish**

**1 TO PREPRARE FILLING:** In a bowl blend all filling ingredients to form a smooth paste.

**2** Working with one sheet of pasta at a time and using a cookie cutter, cut out circles about 2½ inches (6 cm) in diameter. Paint around the rims with beaten egg, then place some filling to one side of center. Fold the pasta over to form a half-moon shape and press the edges together. Run around the cut edge with a zigzag pastry wheel or a crimper cutter and put to one side in single layers.

**3** When all agnolotti are made, heat some oil about ½ inch (1 cm) deep in a shallow frying pan until a slight haze is visible. Fry agnolotti, a few at a time, until golden on both sides. Remove with a slotted spoon and drain on paper towels. Serve warm. Drizzle honey over the top and sprinkle with icing sugar.

**SERVES 4**

# SWEET RICOTTA AND FUSILLI

**½ lb (225 g) fusilli**

**½ cup (125 mL) ricotta cheese**

**pinch salt**

**1 tbsp (15 mL) sugar**

**¼ tsp (1 mL) vanilla extract**

**¼ tsp (1 mL) grated lemon rind**

**¼ tsp (1 mL) cinnamon**

**heated milk**

**julienned lemon rind for decoration**

**1** Cook fusilli until *al dente*.

**2** In a bowl, blend ricotta, pinch salt, sugar, vanilla, lemon rind and cinnamon. Add just enough hot milk to make a smooth sauce.

**3** Drain fusilli and toss with ricotta sauce. Serve immediately, decorated with lemon rind and sprinkled with cinnamon.

**SERVES 4**

# PASTA WITH FRUIT AND NUTS

⅔ lb (300 g) rigatoni or other large,
hollow tubes

¼ lb (110 g) dried figs, softened in
boiling water 15 minutes and
finely chopped

½ cup (125 mL) finely chopped toasted
blanched almonds

½ cup (125 mL) finely chopped walnuts

¼ cup (60 mL) raisins, chopped

3 tbsp (45 mL) marmalade

grated rind of 1 large orange

pinch ground cloves

¼ tsp (1 mL) cinnamon

¼ lb (110 g) butter, melted and browned

sugar

vanilla ice cream, softened

**1** Preheat oven to 375°F (190°C).

**2** Cook rigatoni in boiling salted water
until just *al dente*. Drain, rinse under cold
water and drain again. Stir in a little
vegetable oil and set aside.

**3** In a bowl combine figs, almonds,
walnuts, raisins, marmalade, orange rind
and spices and mix well. Stuff each pasta
tube with filling (use a cake decorating bag
with a large nozzle). Place stuffed pasta
tubes in a single layer in a greased, shallow
ovenproof dish. Pour browned butter over
pasta, sprinkle with sugar and bake for 10
to 15 minutes. Serve immediately with
softened ice cream.

**SERVES 4**

# ALMOND TORTE

4 cups (1 L) milk

1 cup (250 mL) sugar

½ lb (225 g) risoni

3 tbsp (45 mL) vanilla

1 cup (250 mL) blanched almonds

2 tbsp (30 mL) sugar

1 tbsp (15 mL) dried bread crumbs

6 eggs

¼ cup (60 mL) almond liqueur

1 tsp (5 mL) almond extract

**1** In a large saucepan combine milk with
1 cup (250 mL) sugar and bring to the boil.

*Almond Torte*

Add risoni and 1 tbsp (15 mL) vanilla and
boil for 10 minutes, stirring once or twice.
Set aside.

**2** Preheat oven to 300°F (150°C).

**3** Put almonds close together on a sheet of
foil on a baking tray. Sprinkle with 2 tbsp
(30 mL) sugar and some water and place
under the broiler until caramelized. Chop
almonds coarsely with bread crumbs in a
food processor or by hand.

**4** Beat together eggs, almond liqueur and
extract and remaining vanilla. Add risoni
mixture and almonds and mix well. Pour
into a greased shallow 10 inch (25 cm) dish
and bake for about 1 hour, or until the top
is golden brown and the torte is set.

**5** Remove from the oven and immediately
prick holes over the entire surface with a
toothpick or skewer. Sprinkle generously
with additional almond liqueur and let cool.

**SERVES 6 TO 8**

*Preparing Sweet Ravioli*

## SWEET RAVIOLI

**1 cup (250 mL) potato flour**

**1 cup (250 mL) all-purpose flour**

**pinch salt**

**½ cup (125 mL) sugar**

**¼ cup (60 mL) butter**

**1 egg**

**grated rind of 1 lemon**

**3 tbsp (45 mL) milk**

**thick jam for filling**

**beaten egg for sealing**

**1** To make the pasta by hand, sift flours, salt and sugar together and then cut in the butter. Add remaining ingredients except jam and beaten egg and mix to form a dry but pliable dough, using a little more milk or extra flour if needed. Cover and let stand for 1 hour.

**2** If using a food processor, mix dry ingredients briefly (using the metal blade) and then add butter and egg. Mix for a couple of seconds before adding the rest of the ingredients and continue processing until the dough forms a ball and slows or stops the machine. Let stand for 1 hour, covered.

**3** Divide dough into quarters, then roll out each piece into a very thin sheet about

≈ **SWEET RAVIOLI VARIATIONS**

*These ravioli can be served as a dessert with cream or mascarpone, or alone with coffee. They can also be deep-fried instead of baked, in which case they have a crisper pastry, but don't keep. If deep-frying, omit brushing the ravioli with beaten egg.*

12 inches (30 cm) long. Cover with plastic wrap or a damp cloth.

**4** Preheat oven to 350°F (180°C).

**5** Working with one sheet at a time, place half teaspoons (2.5 mL) of jam at evenly spaced intervals along and across its length. Paint between the jam, along the cutting lines, with beaten egg. Cover this sheet with another one and run along the cutting lines with your finger to seal the two pieces together. Cut out the ravioli with a floured zigzag pastry wheel. Repeat with the remaining sheets of pasta.

**6** Brush the ravioli with beaten egg and place on a buttered baking tray. Bake until crisp and golden, about 30 minutes. Cool slightly and serve dusted with icing sugar.

**SERVES 4**

## SWEET CHEESE IN LEMON PASTA

*These lemon parcels can be prepared earlier in the day and kept in the refrigerator, loosely covered, until ready to cook. Experiment with size and shape; they look very good made smaller in a more traditional ravioli size.*

**PASTA**

**2 cups (500 mL) all-purpose flour**

**½ tsp (2.5 mL) salt**

**1 tsp (5 mL) sugar**

**grated rind of 2 lemons**

**3 tbsp (45 mL) fresh lemon juice**

**1 small egg, beaten**

**FILLING**

**2¾ cups (685 mL) cottage cheese**

**⅔ cup (165 mL) sugar**

**¾ cup (185 mL) candied lemon peel**

**3 oz (85 g) dark chocolate, grated**

**½ tsp (2.5 mL) vanilla extract**

**1 tbsp (15 mL) brandy**

**TO ASSEMBLE**

**beaten egg for sealing**

**vegetable oil for frying**

**1 cup (250 mL) cream, flavored to taste with brandy**

**sugar**

**1 TO PREPARE PASTA:** Pile flour, salt, sugar and lemon rind on a work surface and make a well in the center. Add lemon juice and egg and begin blending them into the flour, using a fork. When a loosely combined dough is obtained, use your hands and knead it, incorporating extra flour as you go to form a smooth, dry elastic ball. Cover with a damp cloth or plastic wrap and let stand for 15 minutes.

**2** Divide the ball into four pieces. Working with one piece at a time, roll out to give a very thin sheet of pasta. Cover each sheet as it is completed. Let stand while you prepare the filling.

**3 TO PREPARE FILLING:** Combine all filling ingredients thoroughly.

**4** Cut pasta into 7 x 7 inch (18 x 18 cm) squares. Working with a few at a time, brush around the edges of each square with a little beaten egg. Place some filling in the middle of each and fold corners in, like an envelope, to completely enclose. Press the edges down to seal tightly.

**5** Pour some oil into a pan to ½ – ¾ inch (1 – 2 cm) depth and heat it until a slight haze is given off. Fry parcels, one or two at a time, until golden on both sides. Remove with a slotted spoon and drain on paper towels; keep warm while the remainder are cooking. Serve warm with brandy-flavored cream and sprinkled with sugar.

**SERVES 4 TO 6**

*Sweet Cheese in Lemon Pasta*

*This dish is
embarrassingly easy but
is always a show stopper
when served as the finale
to a dinner party. The
pasta can be prepared
earlier in the day and
kept moist, and the orange
can be grated beforehand,
as well.*

≈ FARFALLE WITH
PISTACHIOS

*This is rich and delicate
and so easy to make.
Sauté 3 oz (90 g)
pistachios in ¼ lb
(110 g) melted butter
until golden. Add ⅓ cup
(85 mL) poppy seeds
and 1 tbsp (15 mL)
sugar and stir to coat.
Toss with ½ lb (225 g)
farfalle, cooked.*

# CHOCOLATE FETTUCCINE WITH ORANGE BUTTER

### CHOCOLATE PASTA

**1 cup (250 mL) durum wheat semolina**

**¾ cup (185 mL) all-purpose flour**

**1 tbsp (15 mL) instant chocolate milk powder**

**1 tsp (5 mL) cocoa powder**

**pinch salt**

**1 egg, lightly beaten**

**1 tsp (5 mL) vegetable oil**

### ORANGE BUTTER

**⅓ lb (150 g) unsalted butter**

**1 large orange**

**1 TO PREPARE PASTA:** Sift dry ingredients together. Gradually mix in egg and oil, adding a little water if necessary, to form a dry but well-combined dough. (Dough can be mixed in a food processor.) Knead dough on a lightly floured board for 6 to 7 minutes to give a smooth and elastic ball. Let stand for at least 15 minutes.

**2** Divide dough in two pieces and roll each piece out into a thin rectangular sheet roughly 8 inches (20 cm) long. Let the pasta sit for a few minutes before cutting. Cut the sheets into fettuccine using a hand-cranked pasta machine, or roll each up along its length and slice off ribbons with a sharp knife.

**3** Cook the pasta in boiling salted water.

**4 TO PREPARE ORANGE BUTTER:** Peel rind off one-quarter of the orange, remove any pith left on the rind and slice it very thinly into ¾ – 1¼ inch (2 – 3 cm) lengths. With a zester or a very fine grater, grate the zest off the rest of the orange, being careful not to collect any of the pith.

**5** In a small saucepan heat butter until it browns slightly. If the butter fats begin to separate, strain the butter into another saucepan and continue. Add orange rind and zest. Heat gently for 2 to 3 minutes until orange rind gives off its distinctive aroma.

**6** Drain cooked pasta and quickly pour the sauce over it. Serve immediately with lightly whipped cream or mascarpone.

**SERVES 4**

# CHOCOLATE NUT CAKE

**½ lb (225 g) farfalle**

**1 cup (250 mL) roasted hazelnuts**

**1½ cups (375 mL) walnut halves**

**¾ cup (185 mL) blanched almonds**

**3 tbsp (45 mL) dried bread crumbs**

**¼ cup (60 mL) cocoa powder**

**1½ oz (40 g) dark chocolate, grated**

**1 tsp (5 mL) cinnamon**

**⅔ cup (165 mL) sugar**

**1 tbsp (15 mL) finely chopped mixed candied peel**

**grated rind of 1 lemon**

**1 tsp (5 mL) vanilla extract**

**¼ cup (60 mL) cognac**

**1** Cook pasta in boiling salted water to which has been added 1 tsp (5 mL) sugar. When it is barely done, drain.

**2** Chop nuts and bread crumbs together in a food processor until a coarse paste forms. Transfer to a bowl and mix with the rest of the ingredients. Stir about ½ cup (125 mL) of this mixture through the warm pasta.

**3** In a greased deep-sided round casserole spread a thin layer of nut paste. Cover this with a layer of pasta, then another of the paste, continuing until fillings are used up. Finish with a topping of nut paste. Cover cake with a flat plate just big enough to fit into the dish, and press down well. Store in a cool spot or refrigerate for at least 12 hours, pressing on the plate from time to time.

**4** Serve at room temperature and decorate with some extra grated chocolate or a dusting of icing sugar. Cut the cake into wedges while still in the dish. Serve with coffee or as a dessert with whipped cream.

**MAKES 12 TO 16 SLICES**

# MEASURING MADE EASY

## HOW TO MEASURE LIQUIDS

| CUPS | U.S. | METRIC |
|---|---|---|
| 2 tablespoons | 1 fluid ounce | 30 mL |
| ¼ cup | 2 fluid ounces | 60 mL |
|  | 3 fluid ounces | 90 mL |
| ½ cup | 4 fluid ounces | 125 mL |
|  | 5 fluid ounces | 150 mL |
|  | 5 1/2 fluid ounces | 170 mL |
| ¾ cup | 6 fluid ounces | 185 mL |
|  | 7 fluid ounces | 220 mL |
| 1 cup | 8 fluid ounces | 250 mL |
| 2 cups | 16 fluid ounces (1 pint) | 500 mL |
| 2½ cups | 20 fluid ounces | 625 mL |
| 4 cups | 32 fluid ounces (1 quart) | 1 litre |

## HOW TO MEASURE DRY INGREDIENTS

| | | |
|---|---|---|
| ½ oz | | 15 g |
| 1 oz | | 30 g |
| 2 oz | | 60 g |
| 3 oz | | 90 g |
| 4 oz | (¼ lb) | 125 g |
| 5 oz | | 155 g |
| 6 oz | | 185 g |
| 7 oz | | 220 g |
| 8 oz | (½ lb) | 250 g |
| 9 oz | | 280 g |
| 10 oz | | 315 g |
| 11 oz | | 345 g |
| 12 oz | (¾ lb) | 375 g |
| 13 oz | | 410 g |
| 14 oz | | 440 g |
| 15 oz | | 470 g |
| 16 oz | (1 lb) | 500 g |
| 24 oz | (1½ lb) | 750 g |
| 32 oz | (2 lb) | 1 kg |

## QUICK CONVERSIONS

| | | |
|---|---|---|
| ¼ inch | | 5 mm |
| ½ inch | | 1 cm |
| ¾ inch | | 2 cm |
| 1 inch | | 2.5 cm |
| 2 inches | | 5 cm |
| 2½ inches | | 6 cm |
| 3¼ inches | | 8 cm |
| 4 inches | | 10 cm |
| 5 inches | | 12 cm |
| 6 inches | | 15 cm |
| 7 inches | | 18 cm |
| 8 inches | | 20 cm |
| 9 inches | | 22 cm |
| 10 inches | | 25 cm |
| 11 inches | | 28 cm |
| 12 inches | (1 foot) | 30 cm |
| 18 inches | | 46 cm |
| 20 inches | | 50 cm |
| 24 inches | (2 feet) | 61 cm |
| 30 inches | | 77 cm |

## USING CUPS AND SPOONS

*All cup and spoon measurements are level*

| | | | | | |
|---|---|---|---|---|---|
| ¼ cup | 2 fluid ounces | 60 mL | ¼ teaspoon | 1 mL |
| ⅓ cup | 2½ fluid ounces | 85 mL | ½ teaspoon | 2.5 mL |
| ½ cup | 4 fluid ounces | 125 mL | 1 teaspoon | 5 mL |
| 1 cup | 8 fluid ounces | 250 mL | 1 tablespoon | 15 mL |

## OVEN TEMPERATURES

| FAHRENHEIT (°F) | CELSIUS (°C) | TEMPERATURES |
|---|---|---|
| 250 | 120 | Very slow |
| 300 | 150 | Slow |
| 325-350 | 160-180 | Moderately slow |
| 375-400 | 190-200 | Moderate |
| 425-450 | 220-230 | Moderately hot |
| 475-500 | 250-260 | Hot |

# INDEX

### DESSERTS
Almond torte 91
Chestnut agnolotti 90
Chocolate fettuccine with orange butter 94
Chocolate nut cake 94
Pasta soufflé 88
Pasta with fruit and nuts 91
Sweet cheese in lemon pasta 92
Sweet pasta cake 90
Sweet ravioli 92
Sweet ricotta and fusilli 90

### MEAT DISHES
Bucatini all'amatriciana 50
Chicken, leek and chickpea soup 57
Chicken rolls with paglia e fieno 75
Fettuccine with peas and ham in egg sauce 50
Ham and mushroom lasagna 29
Lasagnette with chicken livers 40
Lasagnette with mushrooms and chicken 43
Meat roll stuffed with spinach and ham 85
Paglia e fieno with bacon, peas and mushrooms 52
Pappardelle with lamb's liver and bacon 40
Pappardelle with salami 21
Pasta salad with chicken, shrimp and melon 61
Penne all'arrabbiata 53
Pork and veal terrine 73
Ricotta and salami in wine pasta 29
Rigatoni with sausage and marjoram 84
Roast beef with rotelli 81
Roast chicken with pasta stuffing 82
Sauce from Bologna 53
Shells stuffed with bacon, spinach and ricotta 70
Smoked turkey and gnocchi salad 41
Spaghetti with lamb and red peppers 83
Spaghettini with lemon, ham and cream 50
Tagliatelle with asparagus, ham and cream 75
Tagliatelle with veal, wine and cream 86
Tortellini with sausage 40
Zucchini and sausage lasagna 86

### SALADS
Bean and pasta salad 15
Green salad primavera 63
Pasta salad with chicken, shrimp and melon 61
Pastrami, mushroom and cucumber salad 16
Ricotta gnocchetti 14
Saffron risoni salad 15
Salad tricolore 14
Seafood pasta salad 61
Shells and shellfish salad 80
Smoked turkey and gnocchi salad 41
Spinach fusilli and zucchini salad 13
Tuna, green bean and onion salad 16
Tuna gnocchi salad 14

### FISH AND SEAFOOD DISHES
Baked snapper and penne with citrus sauce 85
Bucatini with tomatoes and seafood 76
Farfalle with smoked salmon and mascarpone 54
Fresh herb fettuccine with smoked salmon and asparagus 68
Fusilli and snapper, baked in a parcel 82
Lasagna with shrimp and artichoke hearts 81
Linguine in white clam sauce 26
Pasta with roasted red pepper 70
Penne and fresh tuna with raisin and almond sauce 65
Penne with shrimp and bacon 43
Picchi-pacchi 47
Red pesto 48
Rotelli with spinach and anchovies 38
Saffron pasta with scallops and black caviar 68
Salmon with lemon cannelloni 72
Scallops and roasted peppers with taglierini 66
Seafood agnolotti with coriander and zucchini 66
Seafood pasta salad 61
Seafood with fresh tagliatelle 39
Shells and shellfish salad 80
Smoked trout with fusilli 62
Spaghetti alla puttanesca 48
Spaghetti with calamari 78
Spaghetti with clams 79
Spanish style fresh tuna and lasagnette 74
Spinach fettuccini with anchovies 22
Swordfish with zucchini and saffron 69
Tagliatelle with scallops and smoked salmon 38
Taglierini with sardines 78
Tomato fettuccine with calamari and snow peas 67
Tomato fettuccine with scallops 42
Tuna, olive and caper sauce 38
Tuna and bean salad 16
Tuna and spinach rotolo 64
Tuna gnocchi salad 14

### SOUPS
Broccoli soup 10
Chicken, leek and chickpea soup 57
Pasta and bean soup 56
Pumpkin and leek soup 13
Shrimp and basil soup 10

### VEGETABLE DISHES
Baked eggplant and whole-wheat fettuccine 78
Baked mushroom and ricotta parcels 57
Baked pasta with zucchini and mozzarella 37
Baked tomato sauce 47
Baked tortellini with eggplant and potato 76
Cheese and nut sauce 47
Conchiglie with spinach and almond sauce 33
Fettuccini with ricotta and dill sauce 34
Fresh carrot pasta with cream and mint 60
Gnocchi with fontina sauce 37
Gorgonzola and pistachio fettuccini 33
Gorgonzola and walnut ravioli 72
Linguine with mushrooms 19
Lumache with artichokes 18
Macaroni, cheese and egg cake 26
Marinara sauce 49
Mushroom and spinach lasagna 25
Pasta pie 21
Penne parcels 20
Penne with eggplant and pecorino 23
Penne with leeks, spinach and pimientos 24
Pesto genovese 45
Pistachio mayonnaise 49
Pumpkin gnocchi 27
Ricotta and basil lasagna 64
Rigatoni with ricotta 22
Rotelli with tomatoes and green olives 22
Sauce of four cheeses 46
Sauce of leeks, gruyère and cream 48
Sorrel and spinach sauce 46
Spaghettini with zucchini and walnuts 34
Spicy ricotta agnolotti in herb leaf pasta 58
Spinach chips 28
Spinach pasta frittata 19
Stuffed peppers and tomatoes 18
Tagliatelle and broad beans 62
Tagliatelle with zucchini and basil 59
Taglierini with sun-dried tomatoes and snow peas 37
Tomato taglierini with fennel sauce 30
Tortellini verdi with ricotta and pistachio nuts 33
Vermicelli with walnut sauce 35
Zucchini with saffron sauce 34